SPARKY ... more than GUIDES

CAPITAL RING

Jon Cox
Peter Burton

SPARKY BOOKS

Published in 2024 by Sparky Books

Orders: please visit sparkybooks.co.uk or email sales@sparkybooks.co.uk

© 2024 Jon Cox, Peter Burton

The moral rights of the authors have been asserted.

British Library Cataloguing in Publication Data.

A catalogue record for this book is available from the British Library.

ISBN 978-1-7394112-4-4

Printed by Dolman Scott

05.24

Cover design: Neil Sutton, Cambridge Design Consultants

Design and layout: Neil Sutton, Cambridge Design Consultants

Map development: Haremi Ltd

© OpenStreetMap contributors – The data is available under the Open Database Licence

openstreetmap.org/copyright

Throw-out maps: mapping by Graham Simons; map imagery by ESRI

Contents

The
Capital Ring

Walking gives a unique perspective on a place. The slow, steady rhythm of putting one foot in front of the other, together with the habit of mind of looking outwards rather than inwards, primes the curious walker to notice and absorb their surroundings in a way no other means of moving around the world can.

Nowhere is this more so than in a city – particularly one of nearly nine million people. There is so much to see; so many stories to hear. Getting quickly from place to place – usually by train or bus or car – is the priority for most. Almost everyone in London does walk, of course, but usually as a means to an end; only occasionally to relax and rarely to discover. The paradox of the city is that the range of stimuli is so dizzying that the seasoned metropolitan dweller becomes skilled at filtering the great majority of it out; visitors often notice more.

Whether you are a native Londoner, an immigrant to the city or a visitor, the Capital Ring will surprise you. We guarantee that this 78-mile (125-km) loop around inner London, never more than ten miles from Big Ben, will alter and enhance your conception of London and how it came to be.

The Gun Drill Battery once protected Woolwich Dockyard

This is not a trail that will tell you much about the centre of the city. Had you been walking the route of the Capital Ring a couple of centuries ago, you would have been passing largely through a rural landscape of farms, fields and woodlands, over little rivers, down muddy lanes, specked with villages, with the bulk of the smoky city an ever-present, but distinctly separate, entity in the distance.

For most of its 2000-year existence, London has been relatively contained. Evidence of human occupation along this part of the Thames Valley stretches back to Neolithic times, but London is undoubtedly a Roman city. When Claudius' legions landed in AD 43, they quickly realised the vital role of the Thames to the commerce and communications of their future colony, and, within four years, had founded a town on the river's north bank at a spot narrow enough to bridge. At its peak, Londinium may have had a population upwards of 50,000.

Red Deer in Richmond Park

Walthamstow Marshes

Greenford: unlikely home to London's only beavers

After the collapse of Roman rule in the early 5th century, the city gradually fell into ruins. The Germanic peoples who subsequently migrated to Britain created their own, much smaller, town of Lundenwic to the west of the Roman settlement. It slowly spread, eventually absorbing the Roman city, but it wasn't until late 15th century that London's population again matched that of Londinium. The following century saw the city's first significant growth spurt; by 1800, it was closing in on a million. It

was, though, the coming of the Industrial Revolution and, specifically, the railways that allowed the capital's population to explode outwards into the surrounding countryside. From nearly two million by 1830, London had become home to more than seven million people by 1910.

The London that dominates the Capital Ring is the city created by the Victorian railways and the early 20th-century Metroland of the expanding Tube network. Yet, the city is a historical palimpsest: each era of development overlays the previous one but rarely totally obliterates it. Throughout the walk you catch glimpses of what came before – the old village green, the disused railway line, the medieval palace, the factory, the canal lock, the hunting wood, the steeple, the fishpond, the sewer embankment, the redundant dock. This is a journey through time as much as space, and an extraordinarily varied one.

Woolwich Foot Tunnel

There are obvious highlights: Eltham Palace, Richmond Park, the buildings of Harrow School, the Thames Barrier, the Olympic Park, Syon House. But less obvious delights are also waiting to be uncovered: Crystal Palace Park, Abbey Mills Pumping Station, Severndroog Castle, Wharncliffe Viaduct, Abney Park Cemetery.

There is, inevitably, plenty of street walking and, though this holds interest in itself, there is also a surprising amount of water and greenery on the route. The Thames marks the beginning, midpoint and end of the walk, though you will spend longer ambling beside the capital's second and third rivers: the Brent and the Lea. Then there are the docks, ponds, reservoirs and canals you pass by.

Abney Park Cemetery – arboretum and burial ground

Wembley Arch from Barn Hill

The range of green spaces is notable. The Capital Ring aims to link up as many of these as possible: from extensive ancient woodland to chase and common, park and garden, marsh and wetland, plus green corridors along disused railway lines and atop Victorian sewers. Such environments allow wildlife to thrive. Whether it's the birds of Beckenham Place Park's wet woodland, Richmond Park's deer, the bats of the Hanwell's Wharncliffe Viaduct or, perhaps most thrillingly, the beavers of Paradise Fields in Greenford, the nature lover is never far from an exciting discovery.

Then there are the hills. You may not have previously appreciated quite how topographically interesting London is, but at every compass point of the Capital Ring you are treated to tremendous views. Gazing towards the North Downs from Oxleas Meadow, through the Wembley Arch from Barn Hill, to the south-west from the heights of Richmond Park – all are memorable and often unexpected.

Eltham Palace: Art Deco/medieval mash-up

The route loops through areas that were once heavily industrial – Woolwich, Hackney Wick, Stratford, West Ham, Plaistow. It takes you through a string of one-time villages, some largely unrecognisable as such (Charlton, East Finchley), others very much still proudly distinct (Harrow on the Hill, Highgate). You will witness the full socio-economic sweep of the city and how it has changed (or not) over time: the always high-end residences of Richmond, the solidly middle-class Victorian developments of Eltham, the idealistic Hampstead Garden Suburb, the 1920s cottage estate of Downham, the 1980s Docklands development of Beckton, the currently gentrifying Woodberry Down.

Archer atop East Finchley Station

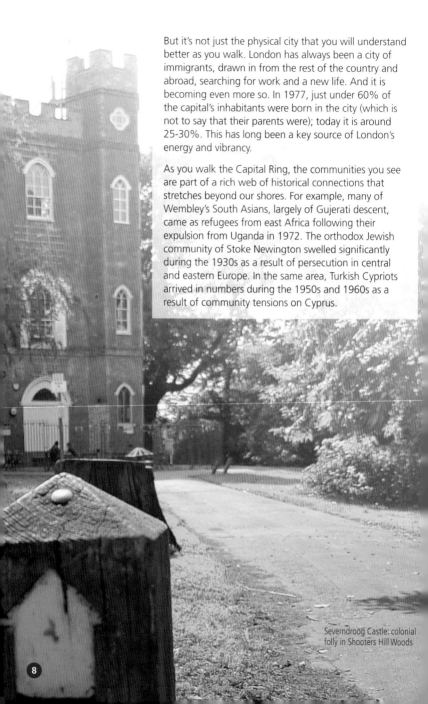

But it's not just the physical city that you will understand better as you walk. London has always been a city of immigrants, drawn in from the rest of the country and abroad, searching for work and a new life. And it is becoming even more so. In 1977, just under 60% of the capital's inhabitants were born in the city (which is not to say that their parents were); today it is around 25-30%. This has long been a key source of London's energy and vibrancy.

As you walk the Capital Ring, the communities you see are part of a rich web of historical connections that stretches beyond our shores. For example, many of Wembley's South Asians, largely of Gujerati descent, came as refugees from east Africa following their expulsion from Uganda in 1972. The orthodox Jewish community of Stoke Newington swelled significantly during the 1930s as a result of persecution in central and eastern Europe. In the same area, Turkish Cypriots arrived in numbers during the 1950s and 1960s as a result of community tensions on Cyprus.

Severndroog Castle: colonial folly in Shooters Hill Woods

All this is not to say that the Capital Ring provides unalloyed delight from beginning to end. There are dull parts. There are scruffy bits. There are sections where you feel you've walked down one too many unremarkable streets in a row. But you're never far from the next positive.

To take just our first stage of the Capital Ring as an example… you will encounter the mighty buildings of the Royal Arsenal, the Thames, a historic dockyard, the Thames Flood Barrier with the towers of the Isle of Dogs beyond, relics of Victorian industry, parks in former gravel pits, a Jacobean manor house, a 400-year-old Mulberry tree, echoes of a riotous 18th century fair, a lofty common, a highwayman's haunt, extensive ancient woodlands, a Gothic-style folly, sweeping views of the North Downs, a handsome 19th-century housing estate, a 16th-century conduit and a medieval/Art Deco palace. Along the way you will meet Daniel Defoe, Frankie Howerd, Kate Bush, Bob Hope, WG Grace, Edith Nesbit and several kings.

Hip Hackney Wick

Could you ask much more from a day's walking than that?

Victorian dinosaurs roam Crystal Palace Park

Development of the Capital Ring

The early origins of the Capital Ring can be traced back to the 1940s. Town planner Patrick Abercrombie's County of London Plan (1943) and Greater London Plan (1944) called for outward expansion of the city to be stopped by the creation of a 'green belt'. One element was his 'Open Space' idea, which aimed to allow the city dwellers to get from their doorstep to open country via a series of green spaces – through gardens, then parks, along parkways and eventually to the greenbelt. Practically, however, the plan hit obstacles. One problem was that walking parkways along major roads might have been feasible with 1940s' levels of traffic, but would be pretty unpleasant today. Another issue is that the London County Council (LCC) had little interest in green links – roads were for cars, parks for people. The LCC Open Space Plan (1951) focussed on green spaces but not how they might be linked.

It took almost 40 years for the idea to be revisited, when the London Planning Advisory Committee commissioned landscape architect Tom Turner to update Abercrombie's Open Space Plan in 1989. He recommended an 'overlapping layers' approach that looked at routes/corridors for pedestrians, cyclists, wildlife and horse-riders, rather than just a single green space layer. The walking layer was the most developed; he created a map of all London footpaths, asked boroughs for comments, then presented it as 'A Green Strategy for London' to the London Walking Forum in 1990. It included a possible 'inner orbital walk' and 'outer orbital walk'.

The idea was taken up and developed over the next decade and the outer route, the 150-mile (242-km) London Outer Orbital Path, now known as the London Loop, was the first to be completed (2001). The Capital Ring followed, officially opening in 2005. Initially, Transport for London oversaw the maintenance of the route, but responsibility has now been devolved to the individual boroughs through which it passes. Much of the monitoring of the route is now done by the doughty 'Ring Ranger' volunteers from the Inner London Ramblers.

London Stadium and the
Orbit from the River Lea

How to walk the
Capital Ring

➜ How tough is it?

As long-distance trails go, the Capital Ring is not a challenging walk. London is certainly hilly in parts, so there are ups and downs, but rarely are they prolonged. Sections can be muddy in winter and after rain, so make sure you have appropriate footwear. Also, bear in mind that there is, inevitably, a considerable amount of walking on roads and surfaced paths, which can be tough on feet.

It is possible to cycle parts of the Capital Ring though it was not designed with cyclists in mind. A few sections – such as the Greenway in east London – have dedicated cycle lanes, but these are the exception.

Large stretches of the route are paved and accessible for users of wheelchairs and people with limited mobility, but there are many sections that will be challenging or impossible without assistance. The Inner London Ramblers website (innerlondonramblers.org.uk) offers excellent detailed advice on the accessibility of the trail and alternative routes for the trickiest parts.

➜ Finding your way

Our detailed maps have been designed to allow you to navigate using them alone if you wish. However, the signage on the Capital Ring is generally good. You will most frequently see the route's round green, white and blue logo, with Big Ben circled by arrows within a directional arrow. They are not always as prominent as signage for other routes, and you need to pay close attention at times to the direction the arrow is pointing as it's not always obvious from a distance. Positioning can vary, but is usually close to eye level.

There are also white-on-green metal fingerposts (sometimes white on a black background in the boroughs of Richmond and Harrow, due to conservation area restrictions), which also often give directions and distances for the other walking routes you will frequently join and cross. At times, these posts indicate the way to the rail link for the official stages, so be careful not to inadvertently follow them if you're not ending your walk at that point. Also, be aware that signs sometimes get turned to face the wrong direction; always cross-check with the map.

➜ How to get there

One of the joys of walking in London is the ubiquity of public transport options. There is almost no part of the route that is further than a few minutes' walk from a bus route, and a train station is usually also within easy reach. All our stages start and finish either at a rail/ tube station or within five or so minutes' walk of one. We list the nearest stations in the stage descriptors below.

Crystal Palace Station

➜ Facilities

There are countless opportunities to refuel along the route, particularly as you pass through the centres of each district. In parts of the walk where options are in short supply – such as in woodlands – we point out if there is a handy café ☕ close by.

Although you will be walking through a lot of green spaces, this is an urban walk and, as such, knowing where toilets are is important. Of course, any pub or café you come across will have facilities, but we have also marked all public toilets along the route with a 🚻 symbol.

Unlike many long-distance walking trails, very few people attempt the Capital Ring in one go. The great majority of walkers do the stages as day walks, travelling home at the end of the day. If you are visiting London and staying overnight, you would probably be wise to choose accommodation in the centre of the city; no starting point on the walk will be more than half an hour's train ride away.

➜ Stages, where to start and timings

As a circular route, you can, of course, start the Capital Ring anywhere you want. We do recommend, though, beginning and ending at Woolwich. London exists because of the Thames, and it feels appropriate to set off from the great river and return to it at the finish. And walking below it through the Woolwich Foot Tunnel provides a fittingly dramatic finale.

Equally, you can choose to walk in a clockwise or an anti-clockwise direction. Most people tend to go clockwise, largely because this is the way the official stages were originally laid out, and this is how we describe our stages below. However, it's perfectly possible to use our maps to walk in the opposite direction if that's what takes your fancy.

When the Capital Ring was devised in the 1990s, it was split into 15 stages, varying from under four miles to almost eight miles. You may wish to follow these 'official' stages; it is very easy to do so using our maps.

We have created our guide, however, more for those wanting longer day-walks, and have combined the 15 official legs into **seven stages** of our own, varying from around nine miles to just under 13, with most hovering around the 11-mile mark. We have walked these seven stages and found them just about right for walkers of no more than a moderate level of fitness. But, as a circular walk, there's nothing stopping you from tailoring your own stages to your own needs. With buses and trains so abundant, you're never far from a public transport link.

The timings we give below assume a leisurely pace of around 2mph (3kmh), which translates at about 5-6 hours walking for most stages. Note, though, that this is just walking time. If you throw in a lunch stop and a little dawdling at the most interesting spots, then your overall time will increase.

River Lea, near Springfield Marina

The following table details our seven stages, together with (in italics) the official stages with which they coincide:

Stages of the Capital Ring

Stage	Rating	Distance	Time
1 Woolwich to Grove Park		**9.8 miles (15.8km)**	**5hrs**
Woolwich to Falconwood	❽	*5.7 miles (9.2km)*	*3hrs*
Falconwood to Grove Park	❻	*4.1 miles (6.6km)*	*2hrs*
2 Grove Park to Streatham		**11.7 miles (18.8 km)**	**5hrs 45mins**
Grove Park to Crystal Palace	❼	*7.8 miles (12.5km)*	*3hrs 45mins*
Crystal Palace to Streatham	❺	*3.9 miles (6.3km)*	*2hrs*
3 Streatham to Richmond		**12.8 miles (20.6km)**	**6hrs 30mins**
Streatham to Wimbledon Park	❸	*6.0 miles (9.7km)*	*3hrs*
Wimbledon Park to Richmond	❾	*6.8 miles (10.9km)*	*3hrs 30mins*
4 Richmond to Greenford		**9.1 miles (14.6km)**	**4hrs 30mins**
Richmond to Osterley Lock	❼	*4.1 miles (6.6km)*	*2hrs*
Osterley Lock to Greenford	❺	*5.0 miles (8.0km)*	*2hrs 30mins*
5 Greenford to Hendon		**12.2 miles (19.6km)**	**6hrs**
Greenford to South Kenton	❼	*5.9 miles (9.5km)*	*3hrs*
South Kenton to Hendon Park	❸	*6.3 miles (10.1km)*	*3hrs*
6 Hendon to Stoke Newington		**10.8 miles (17.4km)**	**5hrs 30mins**
Hendon Park to Highgate	❼	*5.4 miles (8.7km)*	*2hrs 45mins*
Highgate to Stoke Newington	❽	*5.4 miles (8.7km)*	*2hrs 45mins*
7 Stoke Newington to Woolwich		**11.5 miles (18.5km)**	**5hrs 45mins**
Stoke Newington to Hackney Wick	❼	*3.7 miles (6.0km)*	*1hr 45mins*
Hackney Wick to Beckton District Park	❻	*4.8 miles (7.7km)*	*2hrs 30mins*
Beckton District Park to Woolwich	❼	*3.0 miles (4.8km)*	*1hr 30mins*
		78 miles (125km)	

Sparky ratings

You will see a white number in a black circle next to each of the official legs in the table opposite. These are our Sparky ratings: our purely subjective assessments of the range of interest contained within each stage. A rating of ❿ would suggest the most perfect walk imaginable; ❶ would be beyond awful. They do not reflect relative difficulty or scenic beauty but rather the variety of fascinating stuff to be found in that walk.

Any day-walk within London contains such variety that summing it up in a single number is not meaningful or helpful. It is for that reason that we have rated the shorter official stages that make up our day-walks to give you a more accurate assessment of each part of the walk.

For example, Woolwich to Grove Park is particularly exciting for the first two-thirds (Woolwich to Falconwood – rated 8), and still good, but somewhat less thrilling, for the final third (Falconwood to Grove Park – rated 6).

This gives you some idea of what to expect, and also allows those who want to pick and choose which parts of the Capital Ring to walk to make more informed choices.

Stage breakdowns

On the following pages we give you an overview of what you can expect from each of the walk's stages. Be aware that links to public transport options are likely to add between five and ten minutes to your walking time at each end. We also include the nearest rail stations at either end (including to those of the official legs, if you are walking those).

The city from King John's Walk, near Eltham Palace

Stage 1: Woolwich to Grove Park
9.8 miles (15.8km) – 5hrs
Woolwich to Falconwood (5.7miles/9.2km) **8**
Falconwood to Grove Park (4.1miles/6.6km) **6**

Train/tube stations: Woolwich, Woolwich Arsenal,
Woolwich Dockyard; Falconwood; Grove Park

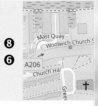

The first stage of the Capital Ring has it all and is bookended by memorable London views. Starting at the Woolwich Foot Tunnel, you are first treated to a riverside stroll from the rapidly regenerating former military and naval hub of Woolwich towards the Thames Barrier. The path then cuts inland to Charlton through a series of parks, including the confusingly similarly named Maryon Park and Maryon Wilson Park, both sitting appealingly within former quarries. You emerge onto the flat, wide-open space of Charlton Park, overlooked by the Jacobean mansion of Charlton House, before continuing through dull Hornfair Park and out onto the wilder expanse of Woolwich Common, with views back towards the river. Crossing busy Shooters Hill, there's the stage's only climb of any note as you rise up into the largest swathe of linked woodlands on the whole of the Capital Ring. Winding through Castlewood, past the delightful folly of Severndroog Castle and neighbouring Jack Wood, you arrive at the café above Oxleas Meadow, with stupendous views south towards the North Downs. You then plunge down through Oxleas Wood and into Shepherdleas Wood, finally emerging from woodland into Eltham Park, which is brutally cut in two by the A2. The path then guides you through the wealthier, leafier streets of Eltham to the medieval/Art Deco treasure of Eltham Palace. As you continue south towards Mottingham the most surprising vista of the stage opens up over horse-roamed fields, taking in the whole sweep of the city from west to east. From here it's a short hop over the A20 and down between sports fields and scrublands to Grove Park.

Stage 2: Grove Park to Streatham

11.7 miles (18.8km) – 5hrs 45mins

Grove Park to Crystal Palace (7.8miles/12.5km) **7**

Crystal Palace to Streatham (3.9miles/6.3km) **5**

Train/tube stations: Grove Park; Crystal Palace;
Streatham Common, Streatham

Workaday Grove Park may not be the most inspiring of starting points, but this is another stage bursting with variety, nature, views and fascinating history. Once over the railway line, the narrow Downham Woodland Walk traverses the 1920s 'cottage estate' of Downham, making it massively more appealing than it would otherwise be. Emerging from greenery to cross the A21 Bromley Road, you're soon plunging into the woods and grasslands of wonderfully diverse Beckenham Place Park. Beyond this, the path threads through the spacious, resolutely middle class streets of New Beckenham and a series of little parks before crossing the railway into the surprisingly interesting, if unfortunately named, Penge, with its fine almshouses. You are now at the foot of one of the Capital Ring's top sites, Crystal Palace Park – dinosaurs, sphinxes, a maze, a proud sporting heritage, superb views – it has it all. Upon exiting, you take a zigzag trail up to and through the lofty heights of Upper Norwood, via Westow Park and Upper Norwood Recreation Ground, before you plunge down through Biggin Wood – a surviving fragment of the once vast Great North Wood – towards a last climb up to the contiguous parks of Norwood Grove and Streatham Common. More fine vistas await you, plus the lovely walled garden of The Rookery, and then a last descent over a grassy swathe brings you to the foot of the Common and the stage end.

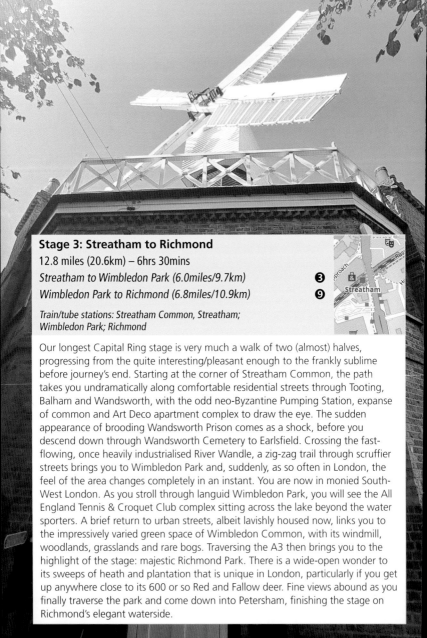

Stage 3: Streatham to Richmond

12.8 miles (20.6km) – 6hrs 30mins

Streatham to Wimbledon Park (6.0miles/9.7km) ❸

Wimbledon Park to Richmond (6.8miles/10.9km) ❾

Train/tube stations: Streatham Common, Streatham;
Wimbledon Park; Richmond

Our longest Capital Ring stage is very much a walk of two (almost) halves, progressing from the quite interesting/pleasant enough to the frankly sublime before journey's end. Starting at the corner of Streatham Common, the path takes you undramatically along comfortable residential streets through Tooting, Balham and Wandsworth, with the odd neo-Byzantine Pumping Station, expanse of common and Art Deco apartment complex to draw the eye. The sudden appearance of brooding Wandsworth Prison comes as a shock, before you descend down through Wandsworth Cemetery to Earlsfield. Crossing the fast-flowing, once heavily industrialised River Wandle, a zig-zag trail through scruffier streets brings you to Wimbledon Park and, suddenly, as so often in London, the feel of the area changes completely in an instant. You are now in monied South-West London. As you stroll through languid Wimbledon Park, you will see the All England Tennis & Croquet Club complex sitting across the lake beyond the water sporters. A brief return to urban streets, albeit lavishly housed now, links you to the impressively varied green space of Wimbledon Common, with its windmill, woodlands, grasslands and rare bogs. Traversing the A3 then brings you to the highlight of the stage: majestic Richmond Park. There is a wide-open wonder to its sweeps of heath and plantation that is unique in London, particularly if you get up anywhere close to its 600 or so Red and Fallow deer. Fine views abound as you finally traverse the park and come down into Petersham, finishing the stage on Richmond's elegant waterside.

Stage 4: Richmond to Greenford

9.1 miles (14.6km) – 4hrs 30mins

Richmond to Osterley Lock (4.1miles/6.6km) ❼

Osterley Lock to Greenford (5.0miles/8.0km) ❺

Train/tube stations: Richmond; Boston Manor; Greenford

This stage, more than any other, is defined by water. It starts by the Thames in rarefied Richmond, and heads broadly northwards, hugging watercourses, to end in gritty Greenford. On the way you cross the often unglamorous suburbs of west London, once hayfield and market garden, on a temporal journey that brings alive the spread of the capital westward in the 19th and, particularly, the 20th century. First, you cross the Thames to stroll up through the quaint riverside village of Old Isleworth and then away from the river, across the extensive grounds of Syon House. The bustle of Brentford comes as a shock, but you soon join the Grand Union Canal, which shares its last few miles before flowing in the Thames with the River Brent, and peace returns. The commercial barges that once thronged the canal are long gone, leaving you with a fascinating 'back door' view on London as you follow its winding towpath under railways and major roads, behind industrial units and along green wildlife corridors (yes, that flash of blue could be a Kingfisher). The canal and the River Brent part company at the Hanwell flight of locks, and soon you come to the arresting sight of Brunel's Wharncliffe Viaduct before passing under it into one of the greenest sections of the Brent River Park, which connects the disparate verdant spaces along the river. You finally bid farewell to the Brent at Perivale Park, and surmount the pounding A40 before a brief and unlovely stretch of road walking brings you to Greenford.

Stage 5: Greenford to Hendon

12.2 miles (19.6km) – 6hrs

Greenford to South Kenton (5.9miles/9.5km) ❼

South Kenton to Hendon Park (6.3miles/10.1km) ❸

Train/tube stations: Greenford; South Kenton; Hendon Central

There are undoubted highlights in this leg's sweep of north-west London, but be warned that there is also a fair amount of up and down and trudging through unremarkable streetscapes. Greenford is soon left behind as you pass through the gates of a beaver-proof underpass to emerge, excitingly, into Paradise Fields, home to London's only wild beaver family. Picking up the Paddington Arm of the Grand Union Canal, you then stroll the towpath before crossing the water and climbing up Horsenden Hill to enjoy the first of several fine viewpoints. On descending again, an unexciting plod takes you through the downbeat streets of Sudbury Hill before you ascend to the startlingly different, rarefied world of Harrow on the Hill. Dominated by its celebrated school and stunning vistas, its villagey High Street is lined with splendid buildings and purposeful boys swishing by in their tailcoats. Yet, before you know it, you are back down in the workaday environs of Northwick Park and South Kenton. It comes as a relief to progress into the tree-lined fields of Fryent Country Park, climbing Barn Hill to admire the closest view you will get on the Capital Ring of the Wembley Arch. More street-strolling through Kingsbury brings you to the last big open space of this stage, the twitchers' haven of the Welsh Harp Reservoir. It's then a final slog across major roads, rail lines and the M1 to bring you to journey's end at Hendon Park.

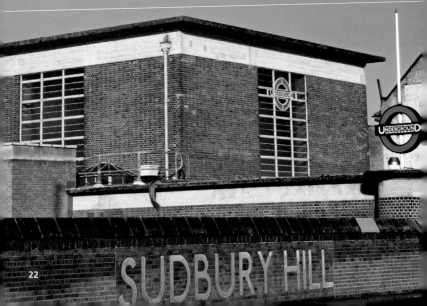

Stage 6: Hendon to Stoke Newington
10.8 miles (17.4km) – 5hrs 30mins
Hendon Park to Highgate (5.4miles/8.7km) ❼
Highgate to Stoke Newington (5.4miles/8.7km) ❽

Train/tube stations: Hendon Central; Highgate; Stoke Newington

This fascinating stage takes you on a socio-economic and cultural, as well as geographic, journey across north London, much of it along appealing green corridors. Starting off in traffic-scarred Hendon, you soon pass into Hendon Park and quickly pick up the rather scruffy but tree-lined upper reaches of the River Brent. As you branch onto the bank of Mutton Brook, the roar of the parallel North Circular eventually fades and the intriguing, slightly surreal calm of Hampstead Garden Suburb appears to the south. A brief interlude of (rather attractive) street walking takes you through the heart of East Finchley before the greenery returns as you plunge through three sets of woods – Cherry Tree, Highgate and Queen's; the latter providing the only significant climbing of the stage. You emerge in lofty, self-assured Highgate, but immediately join the Parkland Walk, another long green passageway, along the course of a disused railway line, punctuated by ghost stations, graffiti-ed brickwork and even a strange creature from Cornish folklore emerging from a railway arch. The scenery changes decisively as you cross the East Coast Mainline into Finsbury Park and then follow the clear waters of the New River as it passes through a light industrial landscape before looping round between the East and West Reservoirs and the huge and rapidly redeveloping Woodberry Down Estate. Journey's end is approaching as you dip through manicured Clissold Park and into the heart of chi-chi Stoke Newington, with a final stroll through the beautiful arboretum of Abney Park Cemetery.

Stage 7: Stoke Newington to Woolwich

11.5 miles (18.5km) – 5hrs 45mins

Stoke Newington to Hackney Wick (3.7miles/6.0km) **❼**
Hackney Wick to Beckton District Park (4.8miles/7.7km) **❻**
Beckton District Park to Woolwich (3.0miles/4.8km) **❼**

Train/tube stations: Stoke Newington; Hackney Wick; Woolwich, Woolwich Arsenal, Woolwich Dockyard

Our final stage takes you on a fascinating journey through the east of London, bringing the area's industrial heritage into particular focus. From Stoke Newington, you are initially street-bound as you head through a solidly Orthodox Jewish residential district to Springfield Park, overlooking the Lea Valley. The historic river's hinterlands are an extensive, evocative tangle of waterways and waterworks, wetlands and marsh, unique in the capital, where biodiversity and human endeavour co-exist. The trail follows the narrow-boat lined Lea for three miles, but the feel of the area changes markedly as you approach the Queen Elizabeth Olympic Park. Nature fades out as you enter what was once a heavily industrialised zone, and its remnants butt up against the shiny set piece architecture of the 2012 Olympics and the colourful, chaotic hipness of Hackney Wick. You leave the Lea, skirting the south of Stratford, but the watery theme continues, albeit subterranean, as you climb atop what is now picturesquely called the Greenway. Once known more accurately as 'Sewerbank', the next three miles of the trail are along the top of the embankment created over the Victorian Northern Outfall Sewer. Past the monumental Abbey Mills Pumping Station, through once industry-heavy West Ham and Plaistow, you stroll until, just as it's getting a little samey, you leave the Greenway to head south through the parks of the relatively modern district of Beckton to the mighty moribund Royal Docks, now home to a university campus and City Airport, and finally back to Mother Thames. An eerie, echoey walk through the Woolwich Foot Tunnel is a fittingly dramatic last hurrah, and the Capital Ring is done.

OLD STREET

24 HOUR
PUMPKIN
PEOPLE

The Maps

The essence of Sparky Walking Guides lies over the page…

Our up-to-date street maps are at a scale of detail that allows easy navigation around the city. The trail is highlighted in yellow or blue to match our seven stages shown on the overview maps at the front and back of the book, and the stage descriptors on the preceding pages.

The maps are equally useful if you choose to walk the shorter 15 official stages. We mark the start/stop point of each of these stages with this symbol 🖉.

The nearest rail link is always visible on the map (and indicated by a green dotted line from the trail). We also include pin markers ✐ every half mile to help you estimate distances. 🎧 indicates public toilets and 🍽 shows cafés away from built-up areas.

You will notice two maps for Crystal Palace Park on pages 54-57, the first showing the direct route across the park, and the second detailing a northerly loop.

What makes a Sparky Walking Guide unique is that we place information on the map itself about what you will see around you as you walk. These bite-sized nuggets aim to explain and entertain, and hopefully enhance your walk. If anything sparks questions or piques your interest, then take a look at the links to related resources that we have included in the 'Get Sparky!' section at the back of the book.

Clear mapping and fascinating facts on every page…our guides are more than just a map.

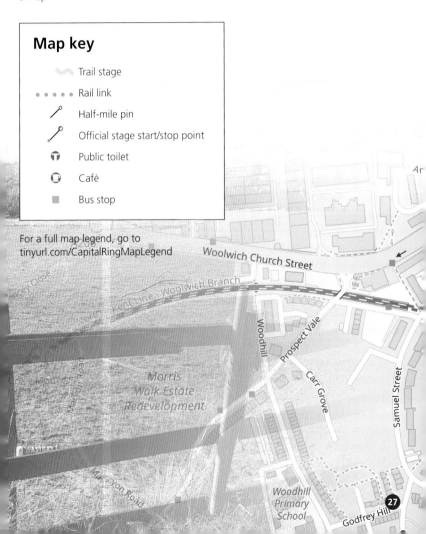

Map key

〰 Trail stage

• • • • • Rail link

🖈 Half-mile pin

🖈 Official stage start/stop point

🚻 Public toilet

☕ Café

■ Bus stop

For a full map legend, go to
tinyurl.com/CapitalRingMapLegend

Woolwich Church Street

Woolwich Branch

Morris
Walk Estate
Redevelopment

Woodhill

Prospect Vale

Carr Grove

Samuel Street

Woodhill
Primary
School

Godfrey Hill

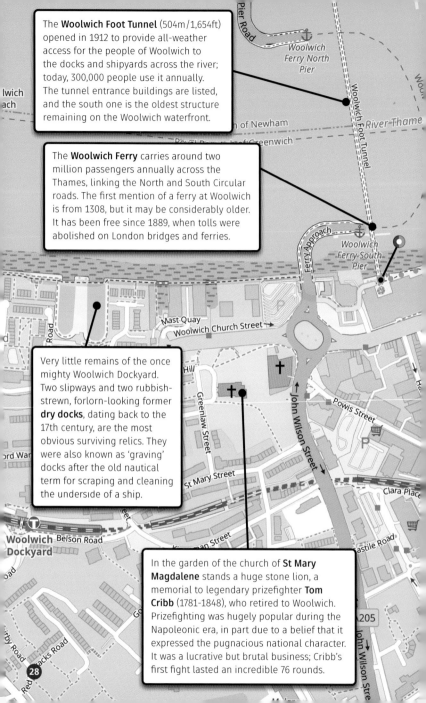

The **Woolwich Foot Tunnel** (504m/1,654ft) opened in 1912 to provide all-weather access for the people of Woolwich to the docks and shipyards across the river; today, 300,000 people use it annually. The tunnel entrance buildings are listed, and the south one is the oldest structure remaining on the Woolwich waterfront.

The **Woolwich Ferry** carries around two million passengers annually across the Thames, linking the North and South Circular roads. The first mention of a ferry at Woolwich is from 1308, but it may be considerably older. It has been free since 1889, when tolls were abolished on London bridges and ferries.

Very little remains of the once mighty Woolwich Dockyard. Two slipways and two rubbish-strewn, forlorn-looking former **dry docks**, dating back to the 17th century, are the most obvious surviving relics. They were also known as 'graving' docks after the old nautical term for scraping and cleaning the underside of a ship.

In the garden of the church of **St Mary Magdalene** stands a huge stone lion, a memorial to legendary prizefighter **Tom Cribb** (1781-1848), who retired to Woolwich. Prizefighting was hugely popular during the Napoleonic era, in part due to a belief that it expressed the pugnacious national character. It was a lucrative but brutal business; Cribb's first fight lasted an incredible 76 rounds.

28

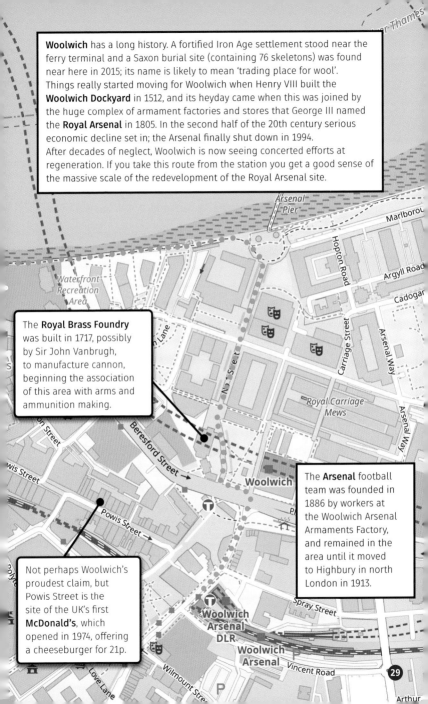

Woolwich has a long history. A fortified Iron Age settlement stood near the ferry terminal and a Saxon burial site (containing 76 skeletons) was found near here in 2015; its name is likely to mean 'trading place for wool'. Things really started moving for Woolwich when Henry VIII built the **Woolwich Dockyard** in 1512, and its heyday came when this was joined by the huge complex of armament factories and stores that George III named the **Royal Arsenal** in 1805. In the second half of the 20th century serious economic decline set in; the Arsenal finally shut down in 1994.

After decades of neglect, Woolwich is now seeing concerted efforts at regeneration. If you take this route from the station you get a good sense of the massive scale of the redevelopment of the Royal Arsenal site.

The **Royal Brass Foundry** was built in 1717, possibly by Sir John Vanbrugh, to manufacture cannon, beginning the association of this area with arms and ammunition making.

The **Arsenal** football team was founded in 1886 by workers at the Woolwich Arsenal Armaments Factory, and remained in the area until it moved to Highbury in north London in 1913.

Not perhaps Woolwich's proudest claim, but Powis Street is the site of the UK's first **McDonald's**, which opened in 1974, offering a cheeseburger for 21p.

29

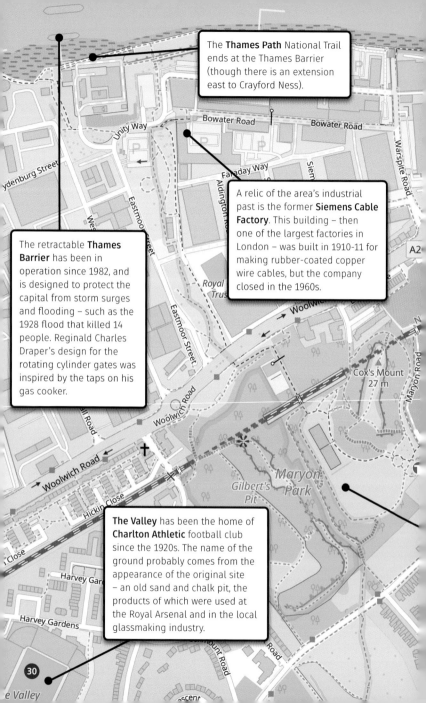

The **Thames Path** National Trail ends at the Thames Barrier (though there is an extension east to Crayford Ness).

A relic of the area's industrial past is the former **Siemens Cable Factory**. This building – then one of the largest factories in London – was built in 1910-11 for making rubber-coated copper wire cables, but the company closed in the 1960s.

The retractable **Thames Barrier** has been in operation since 1982, and is designed to protect the capital from storm surges and flooding – such as the 1928 flood that killed 14 people. Reginald Charles Draper's design for the rotating cylinder gates was inspired by the taps on his gas cooker.

The Valley has been the home of **Charlton Athletic** football club since the 1920s. The name of the ground probably comes from the appearance of the original site – an old sand and chalk pit, the products of which were used at the Royal Arsenal and in the local glassmaking industry.

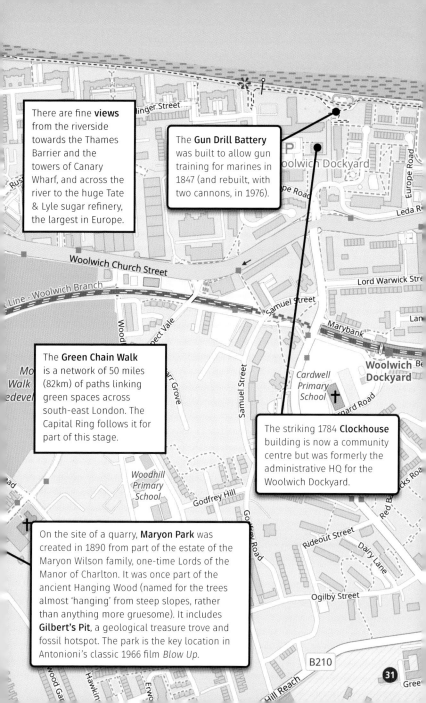

There are fine **views** from the riverside towards the Thames Barrier and the towers of Canary Wharf, and across the river to the huge Tate & Lyle sugar refinery, the largest in Europe.

The **Gun Drill Battery** was built to allow gun training for marines in 1847 (and rebuilt, with two cannons, in 1976).

The **Green Chain Walk** is a network of 50 miles (82km) of paths linking green spaces across south-east London. The Capital Ring follows it for part of this stage.

The striking 1784 **Clockhouse** building is now a community centre but was formerly the administrative HQ for the Woolwich Dockyard.

On the site of a quarry, **Maryon Park** was created in 1890 from part of the estate of the Maryon Wilson family, one-time Lords of the Manor of Charlton. It was once part of the ancient Hanging Wood (named for the trees almost 'hanging' from steep slopes, rather than anything more gruesome). It includes **Gilbert's Pit**, a geological treasure trove and fossil hotspot. The park is the key location in Antonioni's classic 1966 film *Blow Up*.

Woolwich Dockyard

Cardwell Primary School

Woolwich Dockyard

Woodhill Primary School

Woolwich Church Street

Line - Woolwich Branch

Samuel Street

Marybank

Lord Warwick Stre

Europe Road

Leda R

Godfrey Hill

Rideout Street

Dairy Lane

Ogilby Street

Red Ba cks Road

B210

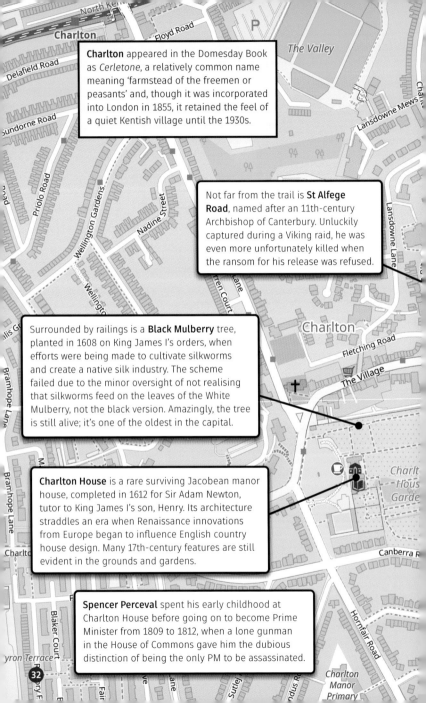

Charlton appeared in the Domesday Book as *Cerletone*, a relatively common name meaning 'farmstead of the freemen or peasants' and, though it was incorporated into London in 1855, it retained the feel of a quiet Kentish village until the 1930s.

Not far from the trail is **St Alfege Road**, named after an 11th-century Archbishop of Canterbury. Unluckily captured during a Viking raid, he was even more unfortunately killed when the ransom for his release was refused.

Surrounded by railings is a **Black Mulberry** tree, planted in 1608 on King James I's orders, when efforts were being made to cultivate silkworms and create a native silk industry. The scheme failed due to the minor oversight of not realising that silkworms feed on the leaves of the White Mulberry, not the black version. Amazingly, the tree is still alive; it's one of the oldest in the capital.

Charlton House is a rare surviving Jacobean manor house, completed in 1612 for Sir Adam Newton, tutor to King James I's son, Henry. Its architecture straddles an era when Renaissance innovations from Europe began to influence English country house design. Many 17th-century features are still evident in the grounds and gardens.

Spencer Perceval spent his early childhood at Charlton House before going on to become Prime Minister from 1809 to 1812, when a lone gunman in the House of Commons gave him the dubious distinction of being the only PM to be assassinated.

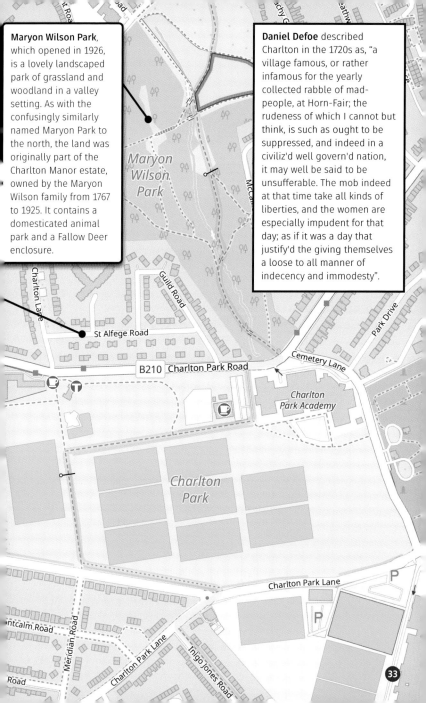

Maryon Wilson Park, which opened in 1926, is a lovely landscaped park of grassland and woodland in a valley setting. As with the confusingly similarly named Maryon Park to the north, the land was originally part of the Charlton Manor estate, owned by the Maryon Wilson family from 1767 to 1925. It contains a domesticated animal park and a Fallow Deer enclosure.

Daniel Defoe described Charlton in the 1720s as, "a village famous, or rather infamous for the yearly collected rabble of mad-people, at Horn-Fair; the rudeness of which I cannot but think, is such as ought to be suppressed, and indeed in a civiliz'd well govern'd nation, it may well be said to be unsufferable. The mob indeed at that time take all kinds of liberties, and the women are especially impudent for that day; as if it was a day that justify'd the giving themselves a loose to all manner of indecency and immodesty".

Maryon Wilson Park

Charlton Lane

Guild Road

St Alfege Road

B210 Charlton Park Road

Cemetery Lane

Park Drive

Charlton Park Academy

Charlton Park

Charlton Park Lane

ntcalm Road

Meridian Road

Charlton Park Lane

Inigo Jones Road

Road

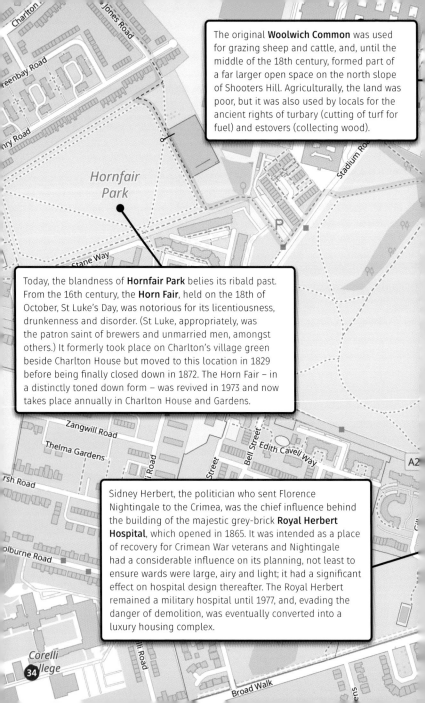

The original **Woolwich Common** was used for grazing sheep and cattle, and, until the middle of the 18th century, formed part of a far larger open space on the north slope of Shooters Hill. Agriculturally, the land was poor, but it was also used by locals for the ancient rights of turbary (cutting of turf for fuel) and estovers (collecting wood).

Hornfair Park

Today, the blandness of **Hornfair Park** belies its ribald past. From the 16th century, the **Horn Fair**, held on the 18th of October, St Luke's Day, was notorious for its licentiousness, drunkenness and disorder. (St Luke, appropriately, was the patron saint of brewers and unmarried men, amongst others.) It formerly took place on Charlton's village green beside Charlton House but moved to this location in 1829 before being finally closed down in 1872. The Horn Fair – in a distinctly toned down form – was revived in 1973 and now takes place annually in Charlton House and Gardens.

Sidney Herbert, the politician who sent Florence Nightingale to the Crimea, was the chief influence behind the building of the majestic grey-brick **Royal Herbert Hospital**, which opened in 1865. It was intended as a place of recovery for Crimean War veterans and Nightingale had a considerable influence on its planning, not least to ensure wards were large, airy and light; it had a significant effect on hospital design thereafter. The Royal Herbert remained a military hospital until 1977, and, evading the danger of demolition, was eventually converted into a luxury housing complex.

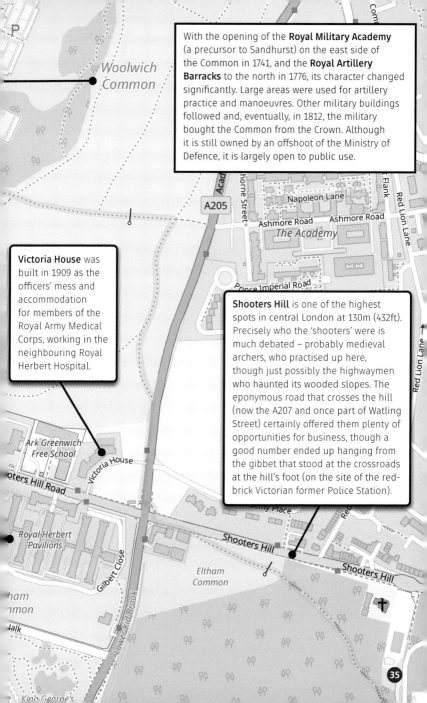

With the opening of the **Royal Military Academy** (a precursor to Sandhurst) on the east side of the Common in 1741, and the **Royal Artillery Barracks** to the north in 1776, its character changed significantly. Large areas were used for artillery practice and manoeuvres. Other military buildings followed and, eventually, in 1812, the military bought the Common from the Crown. Although it is still owned by an offshoot of the Ministry of Defence, it is largely open to public use.

Victoria House was built in 1909 as the officers' mess and accommodation for members of the Royal Army Medical Corps, working in the neighbouring Royal Herbert Hospital.

Shooters Hill is one of the highest spots in central London at 130m (432ft). Precisely who the 'shooters' were is much debated – probably medieval archers, who practised up here, though just possibly the highwaymen who haunted its wooded slopes. The eponymous road that crosses the hill (now the A207 and once part of Watling Street) certainly offered them plenty of opportunities for business, though a good number ended up hanging from the gibbet that stood at the crossroads at the hill's foot (on the site of the red-brick Victorian former Police Station).

Castlewood
and **Jack Wood**
are varied,
predominantly
Oak woodlands
with scatterings of
Birch, Hornbeam,
Holly, Beech and
Blackthorn.

During the 19th century, lofty Shooters Hill was
a desirable location for the homes of wealthy
factory owners and businessmen. A railway
contractor, John Jackson, built **Castlewood
House** around 1869. On the death of a later
owner, London County Council bought the
woods and house and demolished the latter
in 1922. The terrace and some mature trees
(including a Giant Sequoia) are all that survive.

Castlewood

Severndroog
Castle

Stoney Alley

Arundel
Spring

Jack Wood

Arundel Spring

Drive

In 1861, James Wilde, Baron
Penzance, leased 21 acres of
woodland from the Crown
Estate and commissioned the
prolific church architect, Ewan
Christian, to build **Jack Wood
House**. The house lasted until
1926 when it was demolished
by London County Council,
but remnants of its gardens
can still be seen, including
its rose garden and a walled
orchard garden.

The triangular-sided, Gothic-style folly of
Severndroog Castle is a delightfully incongruous
surprise. In 1755, Commodore Sir William James
captured the island fort of Suvarnadurg, south of
Mumbai. When the Commodore died in 1784, his
widow, Anne, had the tower (complete with name
mangled in characteristic Imperial British style)
built as a memorial; the architect was Richard
Jupp, who specialised in lighthouses. It contains
exhibition rooms and a viewing platform with
fabulous views (open Sundays, spring to autumn;
cafe is usually open Thu-Sun). The tower inspired
the 'Tower of Mystery' in local resident Edith
Nesbit's 1901 novel *The Wouldbegoods*.

Westmou

oad

Dumbreck Road

Dumbreck Road

r W

Elibank Road

yhill

Shooters

A popular **café**, with stunning views south over **Oxleas Meadow** towards the North Downs, stands on the site of Wood Lodge, built in the 1780s by the family of Sir John Shaw, owner of the lease on the Manor of Eltham. The Lodge was used as an anti-aircraft unit during the First World War, but demolished and replaced by the café in 1937.

Collectively known as **Shooters Hill Woods**, the adjoining areas of Castlewood, Jack Wood and Oxleas Wood are a prime swathe of ancient woodland. Officially, 'ancient' woodland is any wood that has been undisturbed since at least AD 1600. These woodlands are somewhat older – possibly 8,000 years older.

The most extensive of the woodlands on Shooters Hill, **Oxleas Wood** was opened up for public enjoyment in 1934 after it was bought by London County Council. It's the largest area of ancient woodland to central London and incredibly varied, with 32 species of tree. Oaks dominate but you will also find woodland rarities such as Highclere Holly (the leaves of which are rarely spiny), Wild Plum, and Crack and Grey Willow.

Beware: If coming from the north, don't miss the right turn here. The Capital Ring sign points straight on towards Falconwood, but this is only for if you want to stop at the station. Instead, follow the Green Chain sign (with the Capital Ring logo) for Conduit Meadows and Eltham Palace.

Wogebourne

Crown Woods Lane

Rochester Way

Roche

Shepherdleas

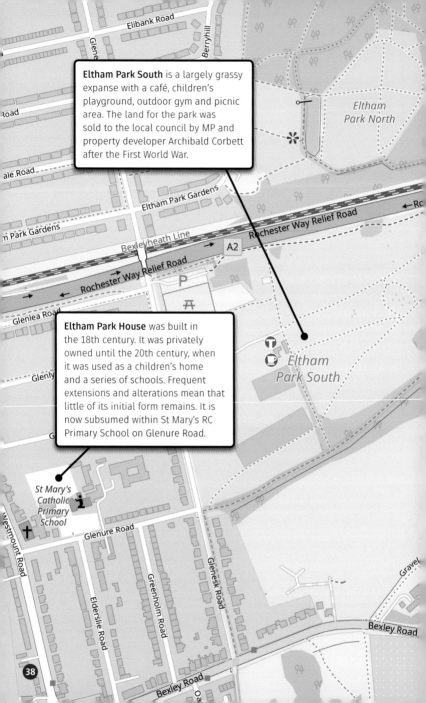

Eltham Park South is a largely grassy expanse with a café, children's playground, outdoor gym and picnic area. The land for the park was sold to the local council by MP and property developer Archibald Corbett after the First World War.

Eltham Park House was built in the 18th century. It was privately owned until the 20th century, when it was used as a children's home and a series of schools. Frequent extensions and alterations mean that little of its initial form remains. It is now subsumed within St Mary's RC Primary School on Glenure Road.

Elibank Road

Berryhill

Gleneagle

Road

ale Road

Road

Eltham Park North

Eltham Park Gardens

m Park Gardens

Rochester Way Relief Road

← Rc

Bexleyheath Line

A2

Rochester Way Relief Road

P

Glenlea Road

Glenly

Eltham Park South

G

St Mary's Catholic Primary School

Glenure Road

Westmount Road

Elderslie Road

Greenholm Road

Glenesk Road

Gravel

Bexley Road

Bexley Road

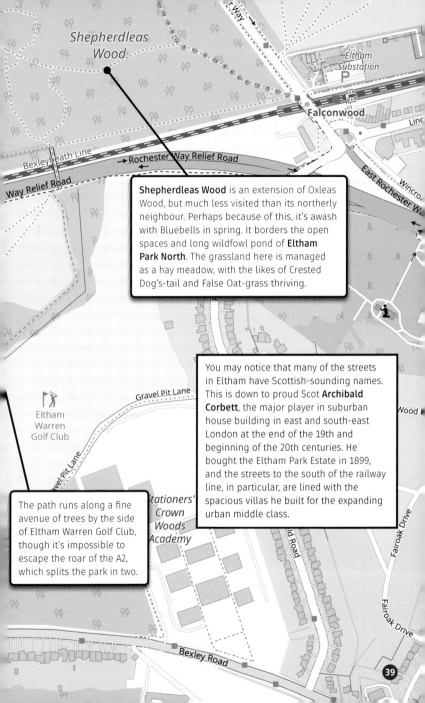

Shepherdleas Wood

Eltham Substation

Falconwood

Bexleyheath Line

→ Rochester Way Relief Road

Way Relief Road

East Rochester Way

Wincro

Lind

Shepherdleas Wood is an extension of Oxleas Wood, but much less visited than its northerly neighbour. Perhaps because of this, it's awash with Bluebells in spring. It borders the open spaces and long wildfowl pond of **Eltham Park North**. The grassland here is managed as a hay meadow, with the likes of Crested Dog's-tail and False Oat-grass thriving.

Eltham Warren Golf Club

Gravel Pit Lane

Gravel Pit Lane

You may notice that many of the streets in Eltham have Scottish-sounding names. This is down to proud Scot **Archibald Corbett**, the major player in suburban house building in east and south-east London at the end of the 19th and beginning of the 20th centuries. He bought the Eltham Park Estate in 1899, and the streets to the south of the railway line, in particular, are lined with the spacious villas he built for the expanding urban middle class.

Wood

Fairoak Drive

The path runs along a fine avenue of trees by the side of Eltham Warren Golf Club, though it's impossible to escape the roar of the A2, which splits the park in two.

Stationers' Crown Woods Academy

Id Road

Fairoak Drive

Bexley Road

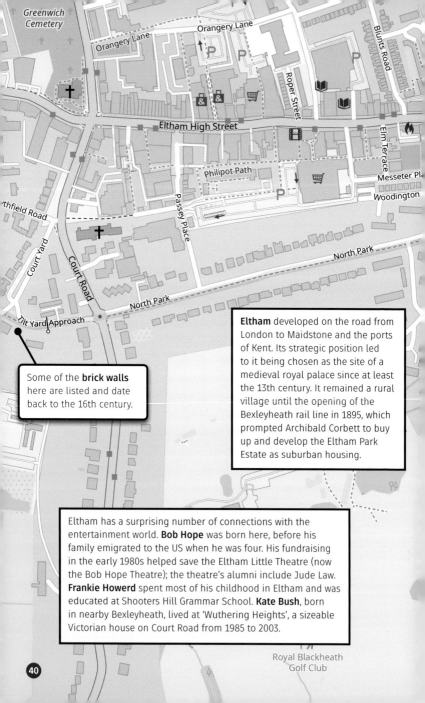

Some of the **brick walls** here are listed and date back to the 16th century.

Eltham developed on the road from London to Maidstone and the ports of Kent. Its strategic position led to it being chosen as the site of a medieval royal palace since at least the 13th century. It remained a rural village until the opening of the Bexleyheath rail line in 1895, which prompted Archibald Corbett to buy up and develop the Eltham Park Estate as suburban housing.

Eltham has a surprising number of connections with the entertainment world. **Bob Hope** was born here, before his family emigrated to the US when he was four. His fundraising in the early 1980s helped save the Eltham Little Theatre (now the Bob Hope Theatre); the theatre's alumni include Jude Law. **Frankie Howerd** spent most of his childhood in Eltham and was educated at Shooters Hill Grammar School. **Kate Bush**, born in nearby Bexleyheath, lived at 'Wuthering Heights', a sizeable Victorian house on Court Road from 1985 to 2003.

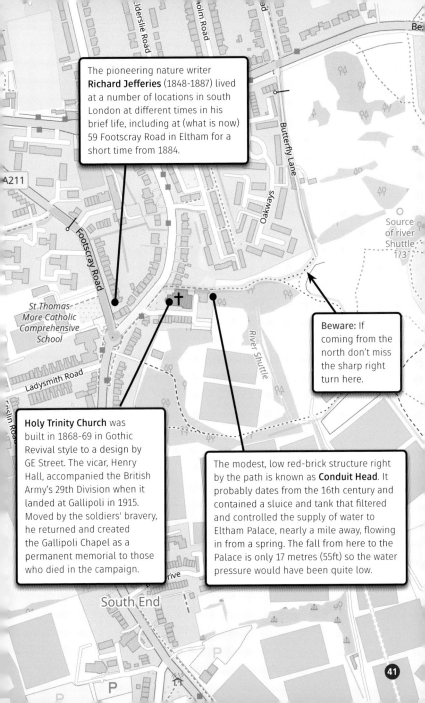

The pioneering nature writer **Richard Jefferies** (1848-1887) lived at a number of locations in south London at different times in his brief life, including at (what is now) 59 Footscray Road in Eltham for a short time from 1884.

Beware: If coming from the north don't miss the sharp right turn here.

Holy Trinity Church was built in 1868-69 in Gothic Revival style to a design by GE Street. The vicar, Henry Hall, accompanied the British Army's 29th Division when it landed at Gallipoli in 1915. Moved by the soldiers' bravery, he returned and created the Gallipoli Chapel as a permanent memorial to those who died in the campaign.

The modest, low red-brick structure right by the path is known as **Conduit Head**. It probably dates from the 16th century and contained a sluice and tank that filtered and controlled the supply of water to Eltham Palace, nearly a mile away, flowing in from a spring. The fall from here to the Palace is only 17 metres (55ft) so the water pressure would have been quite low.

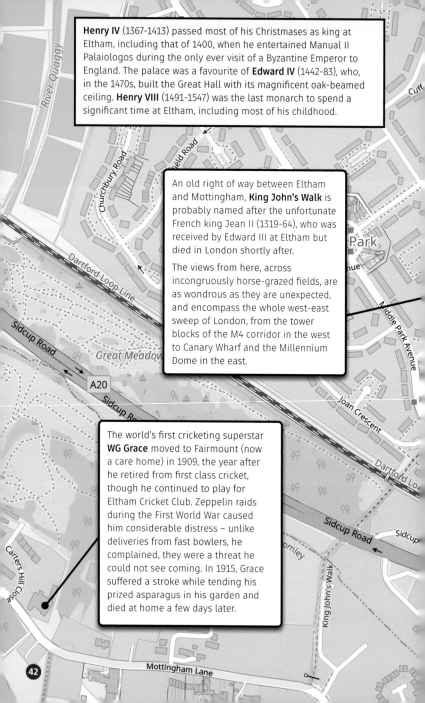

Henry IV (1367-1413) passed most of his Christmases as king at Eltham, including that of 1400, when he entertained Manual II Palaiologos during the only ever visit of a Byzantine Emperor to England. The palace was a favourite of **Edward IV** (1442-83), who, in the 1470s, built the Great Hall with its magnificent oak-beamed ceiling. **Henry VIII** (1491-1547) was the last monarch to spend a significant time at Eltham, including most of his childhood.

An old right of way between Eltham and Mottingham, **King John's Walk** is probably named after the unfortunate French king Jean II (1319-64), who was received by Edward III at Eltham but died in London shortly after.

The views from here, across incongruously horse-grazed fields, are as wondrous as they are unexpected, and encompass the whole west-east sweep of London, from the tower blocks of the M4 corridor in the west to Canary Wharf and the Millennium Dome in the east.

The world's first cricketing superstar **WG Grace** moved to Fairmount (now a care home) in 1909, the year after he retired from first class cricket, though he continued to play for Eltham Cricket Club. Zeppelin raids during the First World War caused him considerable distress – unlike deliveries from fast bowlers, he complained, they were a threat he could not see coming. In 1915, Grace suffered a stroke while tending his prized asparagus in his garden and died at home a few days later.

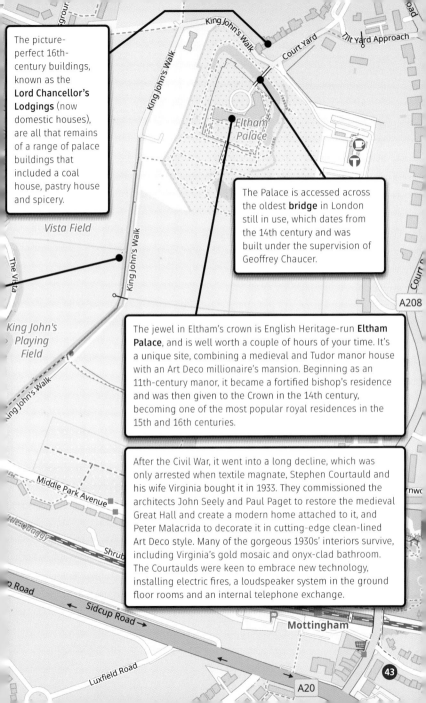

The picture-perfect 16th-century buildings, known as the **Lord Chancellor's Lodgings** (now domestic houses), are all that remains of a range of palace buildings that included a coal house, pastry house and spicery.

The Palace is accessed across the oldest **bridge** in London still in use, which dates from the 14th century and was built under the supervision of Geoffrey Chaucer.

The jewel in Eltham's crown is English Heritage-run **Eltham Palace**, and is well worth a couple of hours of your time. It's a unique site, combining a medieval and Tudor manor house with an Art Deco millionaire's mansion. Beginning as an 11th-century manor, it became a fortified bishop's residence and was then given to the Crown in the 14th century, becoming one of the most popular royal residences in the 15th and 16th centuries.

After the Civil War, it went into a long decline, which was only arrested when textile magnate, Stephen Courtauld and his wife Virginia bought it in 1933. They commissioned the architects John Seely and Paul Paget to restore the medieval Great Hall and create a modern home attached to it, and Peter Malacrida to decorate it in cutting-edge clean-lined Art Deco style. Many of the gorgeous 1930s' interiors survive, including Virginia's gold mosaic and onyx-clad bathroom. The Courtaulds were keen to embrace new technology, installing electric fires, a loudspeaker system in the ground floor rooms and an internal telephone exchange.

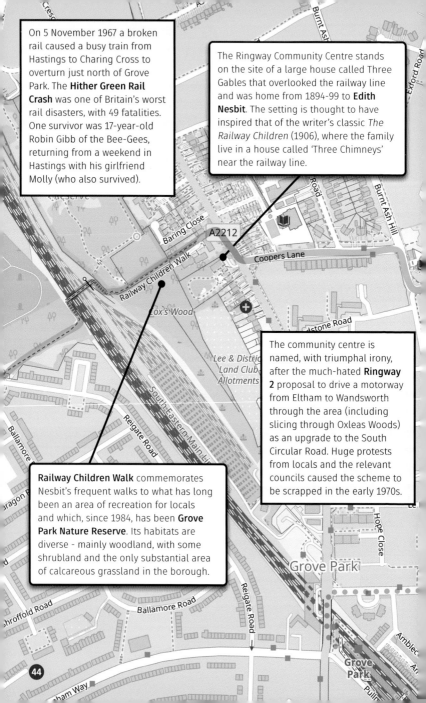

On 5 November 1967 a broken rail caused a busy train from Hastings to Charing Cross to overturn just north of Grove Park. The **Hither Green Rail Crash** was one of Britain's worst rail disasters, with 49 fatalities. One survivor was 17-year-old Robin Gibb of the Bee-Gees, returning from a weekend in Hastings with his girlfriend Molly (who also survived).

The Ringway Community Centre stands on the site of a large house called Three Gables that overlooked the railway line and was home from 1894-99 to **Edith Nesbit**. The setting is thought to have inspired that of the writer's classic *The Railway Children* (1906), where the family live in a house called 'Three Chimneys' near the railway line.

The community centre is named, with triumphal irony, after the much-hated **Ringway 2** proposal to drive a motorway from Eltham to Wandsworth through the area (including slicing through Oxleas Woods) as an upgrade to the South Circular Road. Huge protests from locals and the relevant councils caused the scheme to be scrapped in the early 1970s.

Railway Children Walk commemorates Nesbit's frequent walks to what has long been an area of recreation for locals and which, since 1984, has been **Grove Park Nature Reserve**. Its habitats are diverse - mainly woodland, with some shrubland and the only substantial area of calcareous grassland in the borough.

44

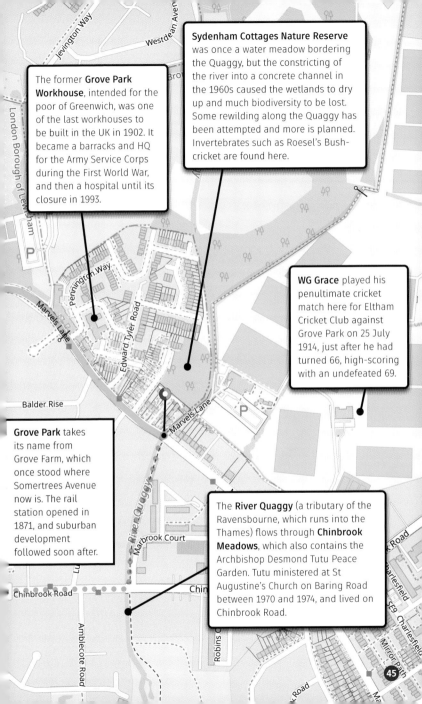

Sydenham Cottages Nature Reserve was once a water meadow bordering the Quaggy, but the constricting of the river into a concrete channel in the 1960s caused the wetlands to dry up and much biodiversity to be lost. Some rewilding along the Quaggy has been attempted and more is planned. Invertebrates such as Roesel's Bush-cricket are found here.

The former **Grove Park Workhouse**, intended for the poor of Greenwich, was one of the last workhouses to be built in the UK in 1902. It became a barracks and HQ for the Army Service Corps during the First World War, and then a hospital until its closure in 1993.

WG Grace played his penultimate cricket match here for Eltham Cricket Club against Grove Park on 25 July 1914, just after he had turned 66, high-scoring with an undefeated 69.

Grove Park takes its name from Grove Farm, which once stood where Somertrees Avenue now is. The rail station opened in 1871, and suburban development followed soon after.

The **River Quaggy** (a tributary of the Ravensbourne, which runs into the Thames) flows through **Chinbrook Meadows**, which also contains the Archbishop Desmond Tutu Peace Garden. Tutu ministered at St Augustine's Church on Baring Road between 1970 and 1974, and lived on Chinbrook Road.

45

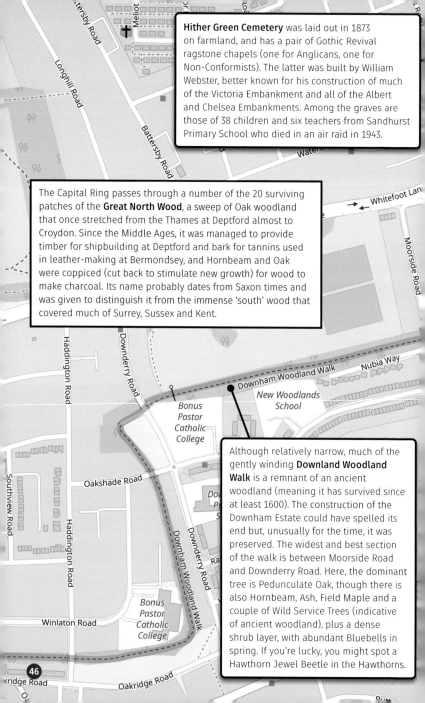

Hither Green Cemetery was laid out in 1873 on farmland, and has a pair of Gothic Revival ragstone chapels (one for Anglicans, one for Non-Conformists). The latter was built by William Webster, better known for his construction of much of the Victoria Embankment and all of the Albert and Chelsea Embankments. Among the graves are those of 38 children and six teachers from Sandhurst Primary School who died in an air raid in 1943.

The Capital Ring passes through a number of the 20 surviving patches of the **Great North Wood**, a sweep of Oak woodland that once stretched from the Thames at Deptford almost to Croydon. Since the Middle Ages, it was managed to provide timber for shipbuilding at Deptford and bark for tannins used in leather-making at Bermondsey, and Hornbeam and Oak were coppiced (cut back to stimulate new growth) for wood to make charcoal. Its name probably dates from Saxon times and was given to distinguish it from the immense 'south' wood that covered much of Surrey, Sussex and Kent.

Although relatively narrow, much of the gently winding **Downland Woodland Walk** is a remnant of an ancient woodland (meaning it has survived since at least 1600). The construction of the Downham Estate could have spelled its end but, unusually for the time, it was preserved. The widest and best section of the walk is between Moorside Road and Downderry Road. Here, the dominant tree is Pedunculate Oak, though there is also Hornbeam, Ash, Field Maple and a couple of Wild Service Trees (indicative of ancient woodland), plus a dense shrub layer, with abundant Bluebells in spring. If you're lucky, you might spot a Hawthorn Jewel Beetle in the Hawthorns.

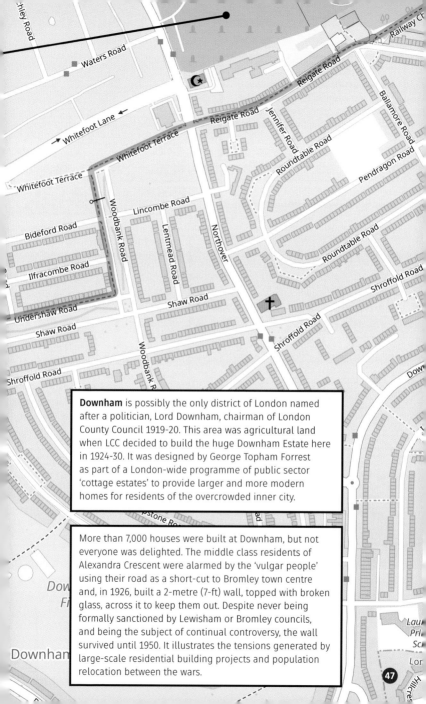

Downham is possibly the only district of London named after a politician, Lord Downham, chairman of London County Council 1919-20. This area was agricultural land when LCC decided to build the huge Downham Estate here in 1924-30. It was designed by George Topham Forrest as part of a London-wide programme of public sector 'cottage estates' to provide larger and more modern homes for residents of the overcrowded inner city.

More than 7,000 houses were built at Downham, but not everyone was delighted. The middle class residents of Alexandra Crescent were alarmed by the 'vulgar people' using their road as a short-cut to Bromley town centre and, in 1926, built a 2-metre (7-ft) wall, topped with broken glass, across it to keep them out. Despite never being formally sanctioned by Lewisham or Bromley councils, and being the subject of continual controversy, the wall survived until 1950. It illustrates the tensions generated by large-scale residential building projects and population relocation between the wars.

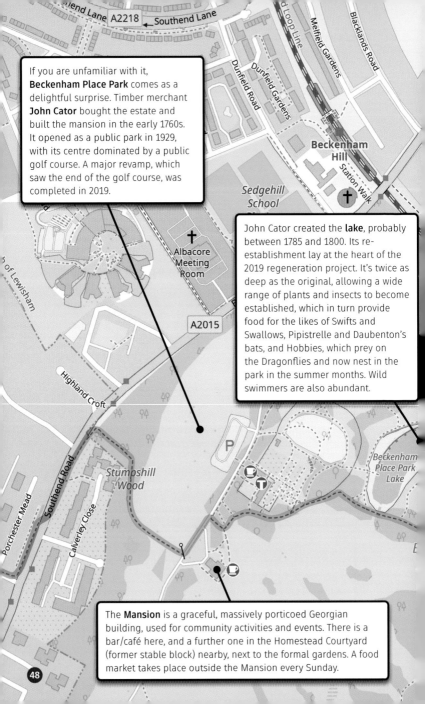

If you are unfamiliar with it, **Beckenham Place Park** comes as a delightful surprise. Timber merchant **John Cator** bought the estate and built the mansion in the early 1760s. It opened as a public park in 1929, with its centre dominated by a public golf course. A major revamp, which saw the end of the golf course, was completed in 2019.

John Cator created the **lake**, probably between 1785 and 1800. Its re-establishment lay at the heart of the 2019 regeneration project. It's twice as deep as the original, allowing a wide range of plants and insects to become established, which in turn provide food for the likes of Swifts and Swallows, Pipistrelle and Daubenton's bats, and Hobbies, which prey on the Dragonflies and now nest in the park in the summer months. Wild swimmers are also abundant.

The **Mansion** is a graceful, massively porticoed Georgian building, used for community activities and events. There is a bar/café here, and a further one in the Homestead Courtyard (former stable block) nearby, next to the formal gardens. A food market takes place outside the Mansion every Sunday.

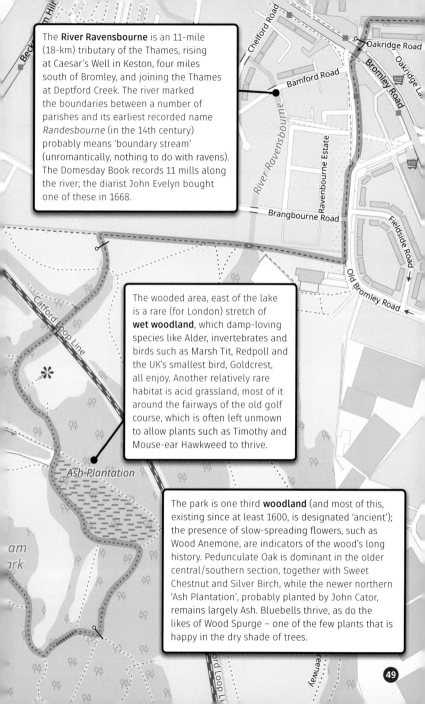

The **River Ravensbourne** is an 11-mile (18-km) tributary of the Thames, rising at Caesar's Well in Keston, four miles south of Bromley, and joining the Thames at Deptford Creek. The river marked the boundaries between a number of parishes and its earliest recorded name *Randesbourne* (in the 14th century) probably means 'boundary stream' (unromantically, nothing to do with ravens). The Domesday Book records 11 mills along the river; the diarist John Evelyn bought one of these in 1668.

The wooded area, east of the lake is a rare (for London) stretch of **wet woodland**, which damp-loving species like Alder, invertebrates and birds such as Marsh Tit, Redpoll and the UK's smallest bird, Goldcrest, all enjoy. Another relatively rare habitat is acid grassland, most of it around the fairways of the old golf course, which is often left unmown to allow plants such as Timothy and Mouse-ear Hawkweed to thrive.

The park is one third **woodland** (and most of this, existing since at least 1600, is designated 'ancient'); the presence of slow-spreading flowers, such as Wood Anemone, are indicators of the wood's long history. Pedunculate Oak is dominant in the older central/southern section, together with Sweet Chestnut and Silver Birch, while the newer northern 'Ash Plantation', probably planted by John Cator, remains largely Ash. Bluebells thrive, as do the likes of Wood Spurge – one of the few plants that is happy in the dry shade of trees.

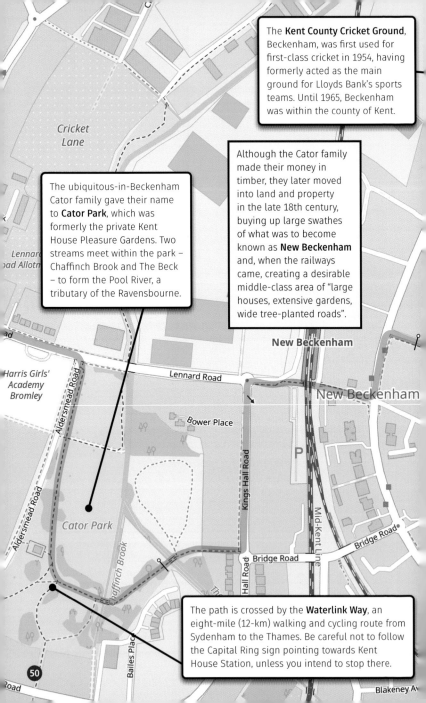

The **Kent County Cricket Ground**, Beckenham, was first used for first-class cricket in 1954, having formerly acted as the main ground for Lloyds Bank's sports teams. Until 1965, Beckenham was within the county of Kent.

The ubiquitous-in-Beckenham Cator family gave their name to **Cator Park**, which was formerly the private Kent House Pleasure Gardens. Two streams meet within the park – Chaffinch Brook and The Beck – to form the Pool River, a tributary of the Ravensbourne.

Although the Cator family made their money in timber, they later moved into land and property in the late 18th century, buying up large swathes of what was to become known as **New Beckenham** and, when the railways came, creating a desirable middle-class area of "large houses, extensive gardens, wide tree-planted roads".

Cricket Lane

Lennard ad Allotn

Harris Girls' Academy Bromley

Aldersmead Road

Aldersmead Road

New Beckenham

New Beckenham

Lennard Road

Bower Place

Kings Hall Road

Mid-Kent Line

P

Cator Park

Chaffinch Brook

Bridge Road

Bridge Road

Hall Road

Bailes Plac

Blakeney Av

oad

50

The path is crossed by the **Waterlink Way**, an eight-mile (12-km) walking and cycling route from Sydenham to the Thames. Be careful not to follow the Capital Ring sign pointing towards Kent House Station, unless you intend to stop there.

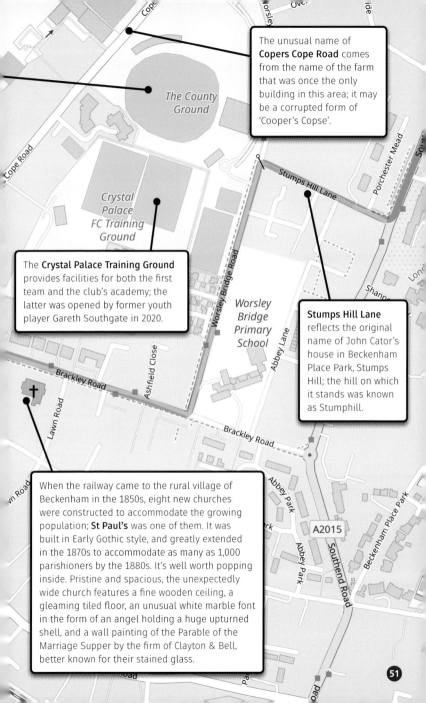

The unusual name of **Copers Cope Road** comes from the name of the farm that was once the only building in this area; it may be a corrupted form of 'Cooper's Copse'.

The County Ground

Crystal Palace FC Training Ground

Stumps Hill Lane

Porchester Mead

Worsley Bridge Road

Abbey Lane

The **Crystal Palace Training Ground** provides facilities for both the first team and the club's academy; the latter was opened by former youth player Gareth Southgate in 2020.

Worsley Bridge Primary School

Ashfield Close

Stumps Hill Lane reflects the original name of John Cator's house in Beckenham Place Park, Stumps Hill; the hill on which it stands was known as Stumphill.

Brackley Road

Lawn Road

Brackley Road

Abbey Park

Beckenham Place Park

A2015

Abbey Park

Southend Road

When the railway came to the rural village of Beckenham in the 1850s, eight new churches were constructed to accommodate the growing population; **St Paul's** was one of them. It was built in Early Gothic style, and greatly extended in the 1870s to accommodate as many as 1,000 parishioners by the 1880s. It's well worth popping inside. Pristine and spacious, the unexpectedly wide church features a fine wooden ceiling, a gleaming tiled floor, an unusual white marble font in the form of an angel holding a huge upturned shell, and a wall painting of the Parable of the Marriage Supper by the firm of Clayton & Bell, better known for their stained glass.

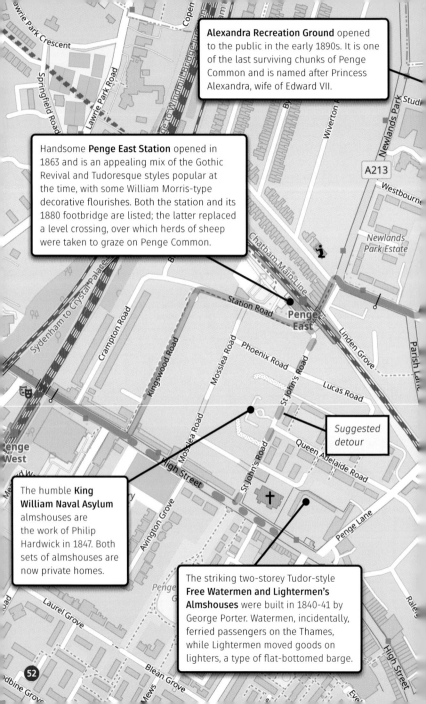

Alexandra Recreation Ground opened to the public in the early 1890s. It is one of the last surviving chunks of Penge Common and is named after Princess Alexandra, wife of Edward VII.

Handsome **Penge East Station** opened in 1863 and is an appealing mix of the Gothic Revival and Tudoresque styles popular at the time, with some William Morris-type decorative flourishes. Both the station and its 1880 footbridge are listed; the latter replaced a level crossing, over which herds of sheep were taken to graze on Penge Common.

Suggested detour

The humble **King William Naval Asylum** almshouses are the work of Philip Hardwick in 1847. Both sets of almshouses are now private homes.

The striking two-storey Tudor-style **Free Watermen and Lightermen's Almshouses** were built in 1840-41 by George Porter. Watermen, incidentally, ferried passengers on the Thames, while Lightermen moved goods on lighters, a type of flat-bottomed barge.

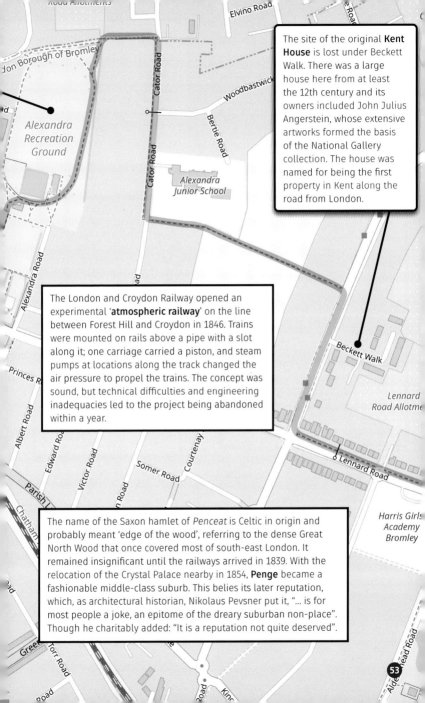

The site of the original **Kent House** is lost under Beckett Walk. There was a large house here from at least the 12th century and its owners included John Julius Angerstein, whose extensive artworks formed the basis of the National Gallery collection. The house was named for being the first property in Kent along the road from London.

The London and Croydon Railway opened an experimental '**atmospheric railway**' on the line between Forest Hill and Croydon in 1846. Trains were mounted on rails above a pipe with a slot along it; one carriage carried a piston, and steam pumps at locations along the track changed the air pressure to propel the trains. The concept was sound, but technical difficulties and engineering inadequacies led to the project being abandoned within a year.

The name of the Saxon hamlet of *Penceat* is Celtic in origin and probably meant 'edge of the wood', referring to the dense Great North Wood that once covered most of south-east London. It remained insignificant until the railways arrived in 1839. With the relocation of the Crystal Palace nearby in 1854, **Penge** became a fashionable middle-class suburb. This belies its later reputation, which, as architectural historian, Nikolaus Pevsner put it, "… is for most people a joke, an epitome of the dreary suburban non-place". Though he charitably added: "It is a reputation not quite deserved".

Joseph Paxton's remarkable glasshouse, dubbed the **Crystal Palace** before it had even been built, was the centrepiece of the world's first international exposition, the 1851 Great Exhibition in Hyde Park. At 563 metres (1,848ft) long, 139 metres (456ft) at its widest and 33 metres (108ft) high in the centre, it was the largest building ever built at the time.

After the Exhibition it was relocated to what was then known as Penge Place on Sydenham Hill. Queen Victoria opened an enlarged version of the Crystal Palace in 1854, with pleasure gardens, including a maze, Italian garden and fountains (with 12,000 individual water jets). It was hugely popular with visitors.

On the evening of 30 November 1936, a small office fire in the central transept (probably started accidentally) rapidly got out of control and soon there were 88 fire engines attempting to put out the blaze. To no avail. The Palace was utterly destroyed.

Crystal Palace Park packs in an extraordinary number of attractions – many of significant historical importance – the park was laid out in the 1850s to provide a fitting setting for the Crystal Palace, and entertainment grounds for the vast crowds who flocked to see it. Although you can just skim the southern edge of the park, it's well worth your time to loop around the whole park; it will add about a mile to your walk.

A pioneering speedway track was built in the park in 1928 and, from the 1950s until 1972, a **motor racing circuit** operated – remnants of it survive as access roads.

The handsome **Crystal Palace Rail Station** opened in 1854 and was one of two stations built to bring crowds in to see the Crystal Palace. The 'High Level' station opened in 1865, but closed in 1954.

54

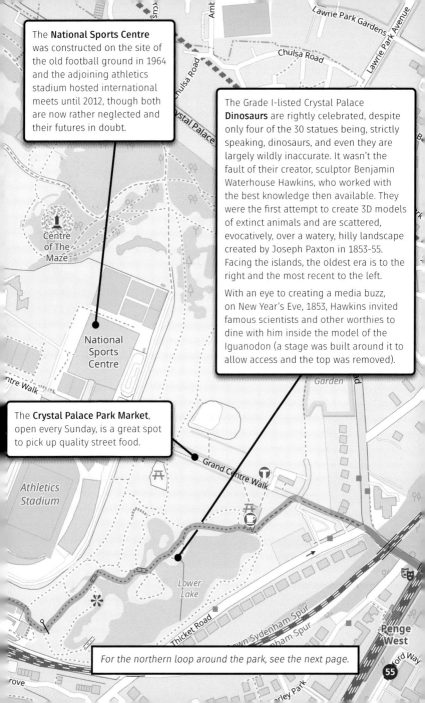

The **National Sports Centre** was constructed on the site of the old football ground in 1964 and the adjoining athletics stadium hosted international meets until 2012, though both are now rather neglected and their futures in doubt.

The Grade I-listed Crystal Palace **Dinosaurs** are rightly celebrated, despite only four of the 30 statues being, strictly speaking, dinosaurs, and even they are largely wildly inaccurate. It wasn't the fault of their creator, sculptor Benjamin Waterhouse Hawkins, who worked with the best knowledge then available. They were the first attempt to create 3D models of extinct animals and are scattered, evocatively, over a watery, hilly landscape created by Joseph Paxton in 1853-55. Facing the islands, the oldest era is to the right and the most recent to the left.

With an eye to creating a media buzz, on New Year's Eve, 1853, Hawkins invited famous scientists and other worthies to dine with him inside the model of the Iguanodon (a stage was built around it to allow access and the top was removed).

The **Crystal Palace Park Market**, open every Sunday, is a great spot to pick up quality street food.

Centre of The Maze

National Sports Centre

Athletics Stadium

Garden

Grand Centre Walk

Lower Lake

Thicket Road

Crown Sydenham Spur

Sydenham Spur

Penge West

For the northern loop around the park, see the next page.

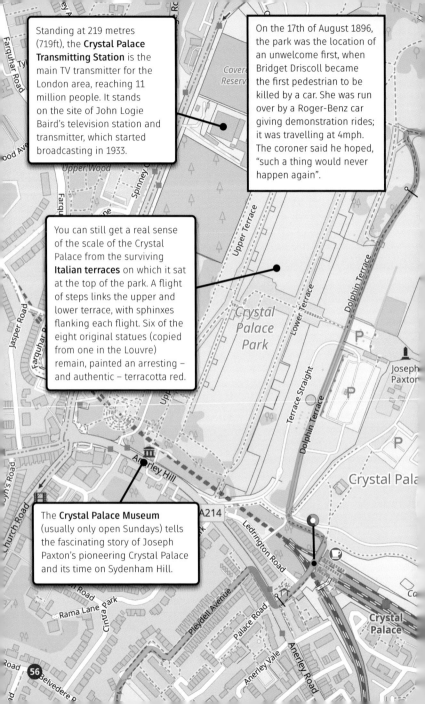

Standing at 219 metres (719ft), the **Crystal Palace Transmitting Station** is the main TV transmitter for the London area, reaching 11 million people. It stands on the site of John Logie Baird's television station and transmitter, which started broadcasting in 1933.

On the 17th of August 1896, the park was the location of an unwelcome first, when Bridget Driscoll became the first pedestrian to be killed by a car. She was run over by a Roger-Benz car giving demonstration rides; it was travelling at 4mph. The coroner said he hoped, "such a thing would never happen again".

You can still get a real sense of the scale of the Crystal Palace from the surviving **Italian terraces** on which it sat at the top of the park. A flight of steps links the upper and lower terrace, with sphinxes flanking each flight. Six of the eight original statues (copied from one in the Louvre) remain, painted an arresting – and authentic – terracotta red.

The **Crystal Palace Museum** (usually only open Sundays) tells the fascinating story of Joseph Paxton's pioneering Crystal Palace and its time on Sydenham Hill.

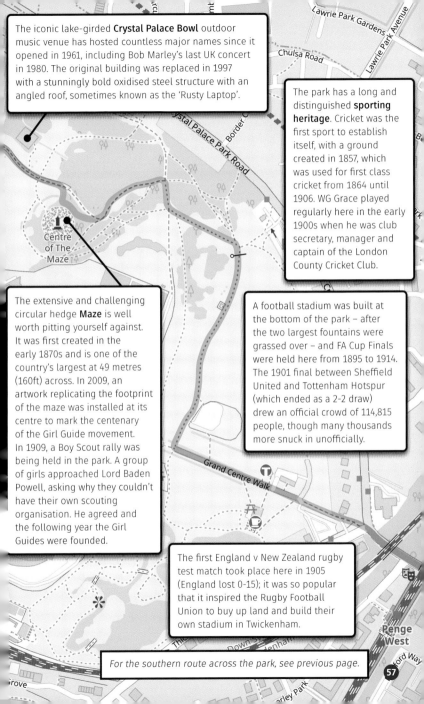

The iconic lake-girded **Crystal Palace Bowl** outdoor music venue has hosted countless major names since it opened in 1961, including Bob Marley's last UK concert in 1980. The original building was replaced in 1997 with a stunningly bold oxidised steel structure with an angled roof, sometimes known as the 'Rusty Laptop'.

The park has a long and distinguished **sporting heritage**. Cricket was the first sport to establish itself, with a ground created in 1857, which was used for first class cricket from 1864 until 1906. WG Grace played regularly here in the early 1900s when he was club secretary, manager and captain of the London County Cricket Club.

Centre of The Maze

The extensive and challenging circular hedge **Maze** is well worth pitting yourself against. It was first created in the early 1870s and is one of the country's largest at 49 metres (160ft) across. In 2009, an artwork replicating the footprint of the maze was installed at its centre to mark the centenary of the Girl Guide movement. In 1909, a Boy Scout rally was being held in the park. A group of girls approached Lord Baden Powell, asking why they couldn't have their own scouting organisation. He agreed and the following year the Girl Guides were founded.

A football stadium was built at the bottom of the park – after the two largest fountains were grassed over – and FA Cup Finals were held here from 1895 to 1914. The 1901 final between Sheffield United and Tottenham Hotspur (which ended as a 2-2 draw) drew an official crowd of 114,815 people, though many thousands more snuck in unofficially.

Grand Centre Walk

The first England v New Zealand rugby test match took place here in 1905 (England lost 0-15); it was so popular that it inspired the Rugby Football Union to buy up land and build their own stadium in Twickenham.

Penge West

For the southern route across the park, see previous page.

57

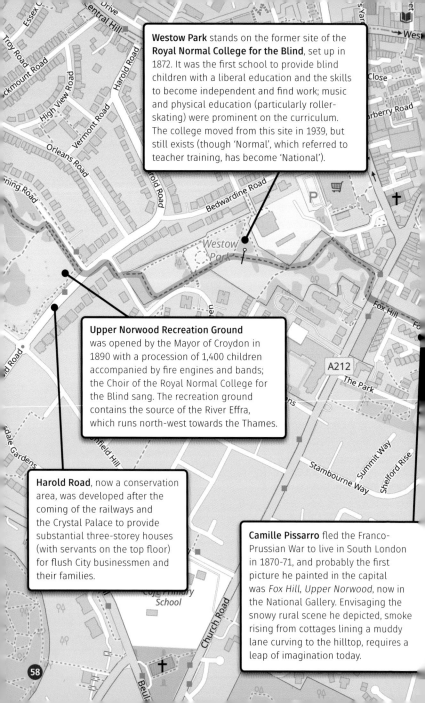

Westow Park stands on the former site of the **Royal Normal College for the Blind**, set up in 1872. It was the first school to provide blind children with a liberal education and the skills to become independent and find work; music and physical education (particularly roller-skating) were prominent on the curriculum. The college moved from this site in 1939, but still exists (though 'Normal', which referred to teacher training, has become 'National').

Upper Norwood Recreation Ground was opened by the Mayor of Croydon in 1890 with a procession of 1,400 children accompanied by fire engines and bands; the Choir of the Royal Normal College for the Blind sang. The recreation ground contains the source of the River Effra, which runs north-west towards the Thames.

Harold Road, now a conservation area, was developed after the coming of the railways and the Crystal Palace to provide substantial three-storey houses (with servants on the top floor) for flush City businessmen and their families.

Camille Pissarro fled the Franco-Prussian War to live in South London in 1870-71, and probably the first picture he painted in the capital was *Fox Hill, Upper Norwood*, now in the National Gallery. Envisaging the snowy rural scene he depicted, smoke rising from cottages lining a muddy lane curving to the hilltop, requires a leap of imagination today.

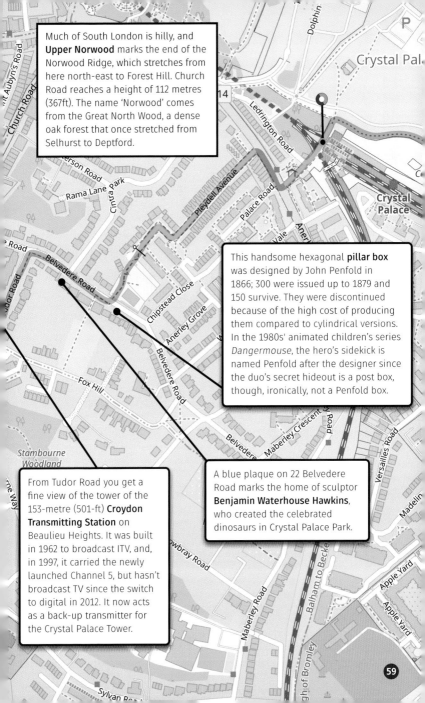

Much of South London is hilly, and **Upper Norwood** marks the end of the Norwood Ridge, which stretches from here north-east to Forest Hill. Church Road reaches a height of 112 metres (367ft). The name 'Norwood' comes from the Great North Wood, a dense oak forest that once stretched from Selhurst to Deptford.

This handsome hexagonal **pillar box** was designed by John Penfold in 1866; 300 were issued up to 1879 and 150 survive. They were discontinued because of the high cost of producing them compared to cylindrical versions. In the 1980s' animated children's series *Dangermouse*, the hero's sidekick is named Penfold after the designer since the duo's secret hideout is a post box, though, ironically, not a Penfold box.

From Tudor Road you get a fine view of the tower of the 153-metre (501-ft) **Croydon Transmitting Station** on Beaulieu Heights. It was built in 1962 to broadcast ITV, and, in 1997, it carried the newly launched Channel 5, but hasn't broadcast TV since the switch to digital in 2012. It now acts as a back-up transmitter for the Crystal Palace Tower.

A blue plaque on 22 Belvedere Road marks the home of sculptor **Benjamin Waterhouse Hawkins**, who created the celebrated dinosaurs in Crystal Palace Park.

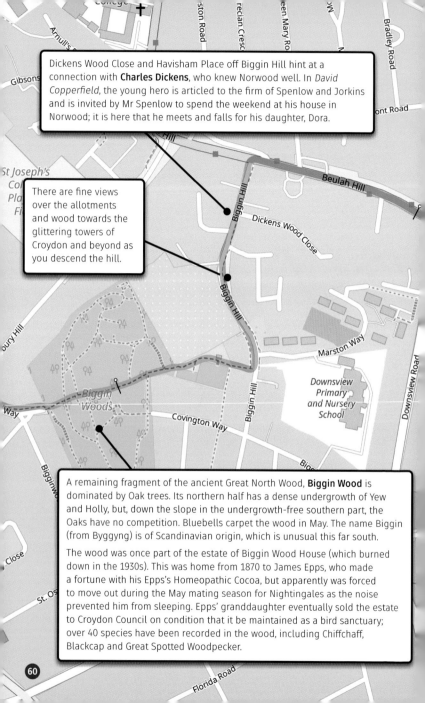

Dickens Wood Close and Havisham Place off Biggin Hill hint at a connection with **Charles Dickens**, who knew Norwood well. In *David Copperfield*, the young hero is articled to the firm of Spenlow and Jorkins and is invited by Mr Spenlow to spend the weekend at his house in Norwood; it is here that he meets and falls for his daughter, Dora.

There are fine views over the allotments and wood towards the glittering towers of Croydon and beyond as you descend the hill.

A remaining fragment of the ancient Great North Wood, **Biggin Wood** is dominated by Oak trees. Its northern half has a dense undergrowth of Yew and Holly, but, down the slope in the undergrowth-free southern part, the Oaks have no competition. Bluebells carpet the wood in May. The name Biggin (from Byggyng) is of Scandinavian origin, which is unusual this far south.

The wood was once part of the estate of Biggin Wood House (which burned down in the 1930s). This was home from 1870 to James Epps, who made a fortune with his Epps's Homeopathic Cocoa, but apparently was forced to move out during the May mating season for Nightingales as the noise prevented him from sleeping. Epps' granddaughter eventually sold the estate to Croydon Council on condition that it be maintained as a bird sanctuary; over 40 species have been recorded in the wood, including Chiffchaff, Blackcap and Great Spotted Woodpecker.

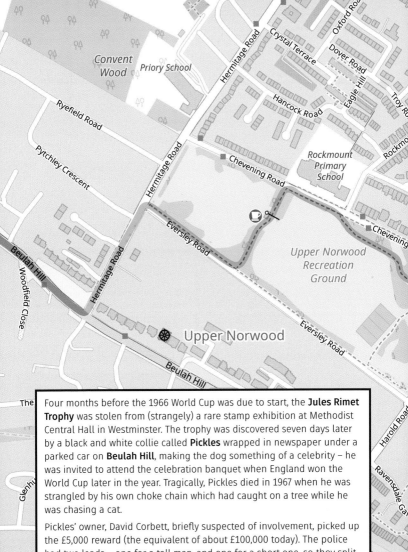

Four months before the 1966 World Cup was due to start, the **Jules Rimet Trophy** was stolen from (strangely) a rare stamp exhibition at Methodist Central Hall in Westminster. The trophy was discovered seven days later by a black and white collie called **Pickles** wrapped in newspaper under a parked car on **Beulah Hill**, making the dog something of a celebrity – he was invited to attend the celebration banquet when England won the World Cup later in the year. Tragically, Pickles died in 1967 when he was strangled by his own choke chain which had caught on a tree while he was chasing a cat.

Pickles' owner, David Corbett, briefly suspected of involvement, picked up the £5,000 reward (the equivalent of about £100,000 today). The police had two leads – one for a tall man, and one for a short one, so they split the difference and put out a description for a person of average height. No-one was ever charged with the theft and it emerged in 2017 that the real culprit was a south London villain called Sidney Cugullere who, according to his nephew, has swiped the trophy "for the thrill".

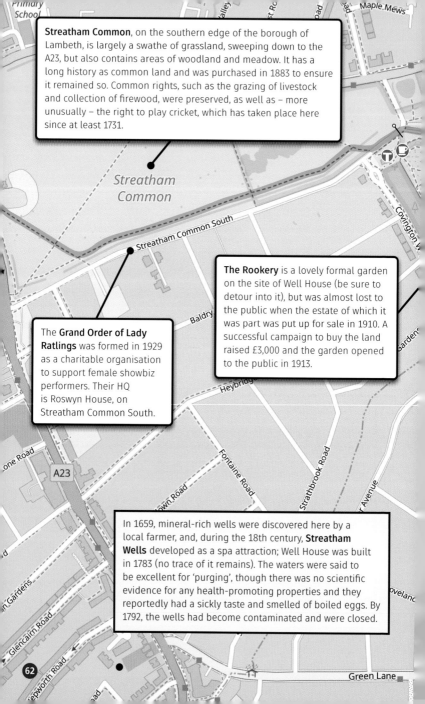

Streatham Common, on the southern edge of the borough of Lambeth, is largely a swathe of grassland, sweeping down to the A23, but also contains areas of woodland and meadow. It has a long history as common land and was purchased in 1883 to ensure it remained so. Common rights, such as the grazing of livestock and collection of firewood, were preserved, as well as – more unusually – the right to play cricket, which has taken place here since at least 1731.

Streatham Common

Streatham Common South

The Rookery is a lovely formal garden on the site of Well House (be sure to detour into it), but was almost lost to the public when the estate of which it was part was put up for sale in 1910. A successful campaign to buy the land raised £3,000 and the garden opened to the public in 1913.

The **Grand Order of Lady Ratlings** was formed in 1929 as a charitable organisation to support female showbiz performers. Their HQ is Roswyn House, on Streatham Common South.

In 1659, mineral-rich wells were discovered here by a local farmer, and, during the 18th century, **Streatham Wells** developed as a spa attraction; Well House was built in 1783 (no trace of it remains). The waters were said to be excellent for 'purging', though there was no scientific evidence for any health-promoting properties and they reportedly had a sickly taste and smelled of boiled eggs. By 1792, the wells had become contaminated and were closed.

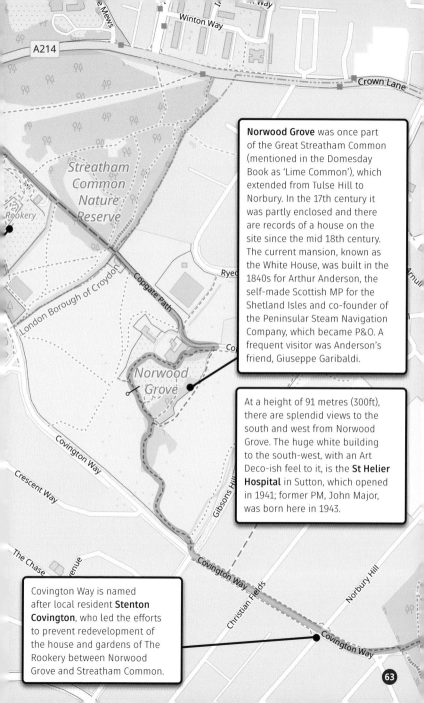

Norwood Grove was once part of the Great Streatham Common (mentioned in the Domesday Book as 'Lime Common'), which extended from Tulse Hill to Norbury. In the 17th century it was partly enclosed and there are records of a house on the site since the mid 18th century. The current mansion, known as the White House, was built in the 1840s for Arthur Anderson, the self-made Scottish MP for the Shetland Isles and co-founder of the Peninsular Steam Navigation Company, which became P&O. A frequent visitor was Anderson's friend, Giuseppe Garibaldi.

At a height of 91 metres (300ft), there are splendid views to the south and west from Norwood Grove. The huge white building to the south-west, with an Art Deco-ish feel to it, is the **St Helier Hospital** in Sutton, which opened in 1941; former PM, John Major, was born here in 1943.

Covington Way is named after local resident **Stenton Covington**, who led the efforts to prevent redevelopment of the house and gardens of The Rookery between Norwood Grove and Streatham Common.

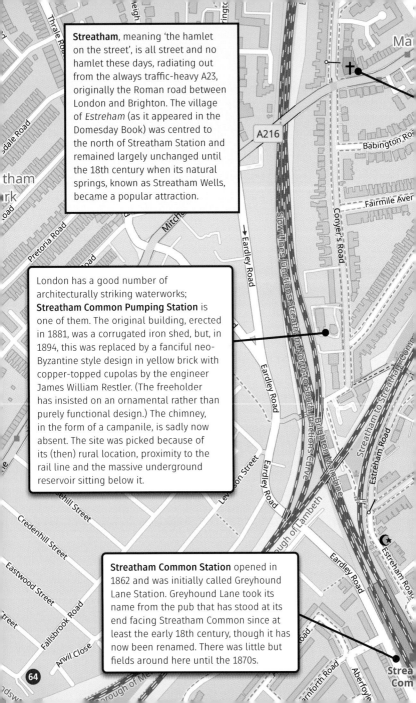

Streatham, meaning 'the hamlet on the street', is all street and no hamlet these days, radiating out from the always traffic-heavy A23, originally the Roman road between London and Brighton. The village of *Estreham* (as it appeared in the Domesday Book) was centred to the north of Streatham Station and remained largely unchanged until the 18th century when its natural springs, known as Streatham Wells, became a popular attraction.

London has a good number of architecturally striking waterworks; **Streatham Common Pumping Station** is one of them. The original building, erected in 1881, was a corrugated iron shed, but, in 1894, this was replaced by a fanciful neo-Byzantine style design in yellow brick with copper-topped cupolas by the engineer James William Restler. (The freeholder has insisted on an ornamental rather than purely functional design.) The chimney, in the form of a campanile, is sadly now absent. The site was picked because of its (then) rural location, proximity to the rail line and the massive underground reservoir sitting below it.

Streatham Common Station opened in 1862 and was initially called Greyhound Lane Station. Greyhound Lane took its name from the pub that has stood at its end facing Streatham Common since at least the early 18th century, though it has now been renamed. There was little but fields around here until the 1870s.

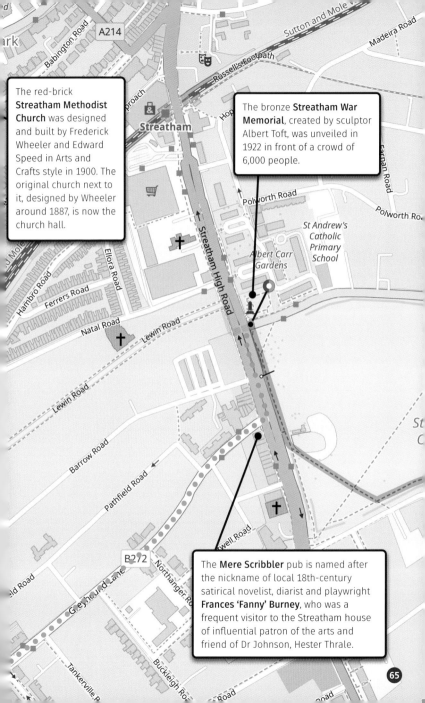

The red-brick **Streatham Methodist Church** was designed and built by Frederick Wheeler and Edward Speed in Arts and Crafts style in 1900. The original church next to it, designed by Wheeler around 1887, is now the church hall.

The bronze **Streatham War Memorial**, created by sculptor Albert Toft, was unveiled in 1922 in front of a crowd of 6,000 people.

The **Mere Scribbler** pub is named after the nickname of local 18th-century satirical novelist, diarist and playwright **Frances 'Fanny' Burney**, who was a frequent visitor to the Streatham house of influential patron of the arts and friend of Dr Johnson, Hester Thrale.

A214

Babington Road

Sutton and Mole

Madeira Road

Russell's Footpath

Streatham

Streatham High Road

Polworth Road

Polworth Ro.

St Andrew's Catholic Primary School

Albert Carr Gardens

Farnan Road

Hambro Road

Ferrers Road

Ellora Road

Natal Road

Lewin Road

Lewin Road

Lewin Road

Barrow Road

Pathfield Road

B272

Northanger Road

Greyhound Lane

Buckleigh Ro

Tankerville R

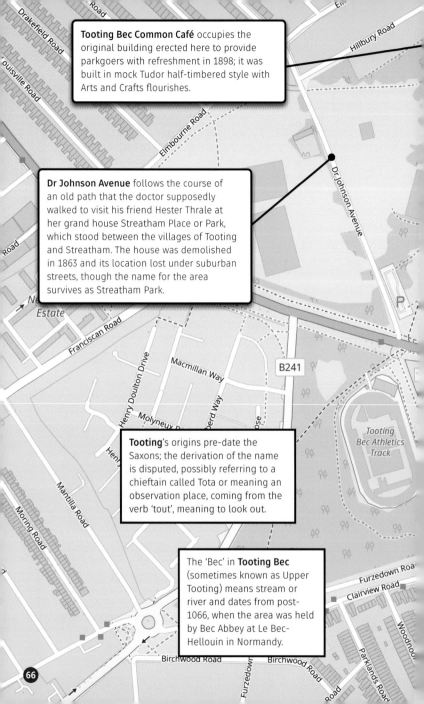

Tooting Bec Common Café occupies the original building erected here to provide parkgoers with refreshment in 1898; it was built in mock Tudor half-timbered style with Arts and Crafts flourishes.

Dr Johnson Avenue follows the course of an old path that the doctor supposedly walked to visit his friend Hester Thrale at her grand house Streatham Place or Park, which stood between the villages of Tooting and Streatham. The house was demolished in 1863 and its location lost under suburban streets, though the name for the area survives as Streatham Park.

Tooting's origins pre-date the Saxons; the derivation of the name is disputed, possibly referring to a chieftain called Tota or meaning an observation place, coming from the verb 'tout', meaning to look out.

The 'Bec' in **Tooting Bec** (sometimes known as Upper Tooting) means stream or river and dates from post-1066, when the area was held by Bec Abbey at Le Bec-Hellouin in Normandy.

Tooting Bec Athletics Track

B241

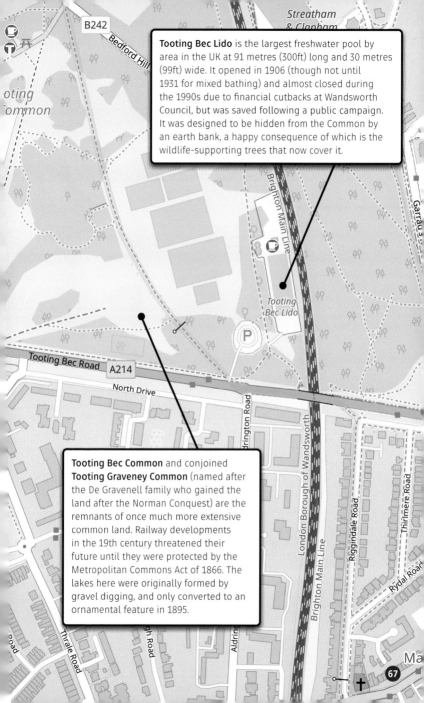

Tooting Bec Lido is the largest freshwater pool by area in the UK at 91 metres (300ft) long and 30 metres (99ft) wide. It opened in 1906 (though not until 1931 for mixed bathing) and almost closed during the 1990s due to financial cutbacks at Wandsworth Council, but was saved following a public campaign. It was designed to be hidden from the Common by an earth bank, a happy consequence of which is the wildlife-supporting trees that now cover it.

Tooting Bec Common and conjoined **Tooting Graveney Common** (named after the De Gravenell family who gained the land after the Norman Conquest) are the remnants of once much more extensive common land. Railway developments in the 19th century threatened their future until they were protected by the Metropolitan Commons Act of 1866. The lakes here were originally formed by gravel digging, and only converted to an ornamental feature in 1895.

Streatham & Clapham

B242

Bedford Hill

oting ommon

Brighton Main Line

Garrau 3.

Tooting Bec Lido

Tooting Bec Road   A214

North Drive

rrington Road

London Borough of Wandsworth

Brighton Main Line

Riggindale Road

Thirlmere Road

Rydal Road

North Drive

Thrale Road

gh Road

Aldring

Ma

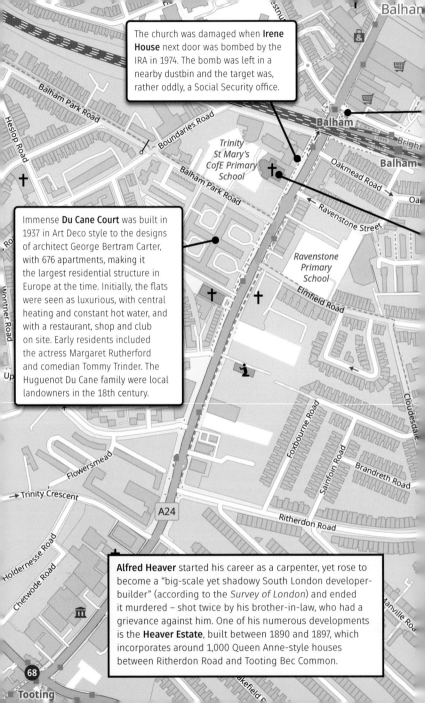

The church was damaged when **Irene House** next door was bombed by the IRA in 1974. The bomb was left in a nearby dustbin and the target was, rather oddly, a Social Security office.

Immense **Du Cane Court** was built in 1937 in Art Deco style to the designs of architect George Bertram Carter, with 676 apartments, making it the largest residential structure in Europe at the time. Initially, the flats were seen as luxurious, with central heating and constant hot water, and with a restaurant, shop and club on site. Early residents included the actress Margaret Rutherford and comedian Tommy Trinder. The Huguenot Du Cane family were local landowners in the 18th century.

Alfred Heaver started his career as a carpenter, yet rose to become a "big-scale yet shadowy South London developer-builder" (according to the *Survey of London*) and ended it murdered – shot twice by his brother-in-law, who had a grievance against him. One of his numerous developments is the **Heaver Estate**, built between 1890 and 1897, which incorporates around 1,000 Queen Anne-style houses between Ritherdon Road and Tooting Bec Common.

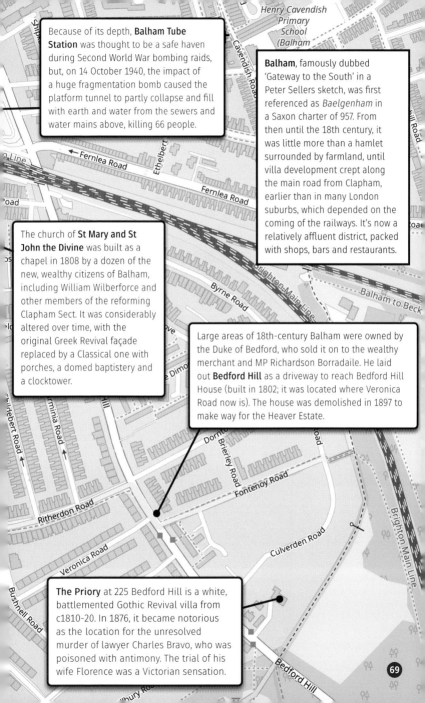

Because of its depth, **Balham Tube Station** was thought to be a safe haven during Second World War bombing raids, but, on 14 October 1940, the impact of a huge fragmentation bomb caused the platform tunnel to partly collapse and fill with earth and water from the sewers and water mains above, killing 66 people.

Balham, famously dubbed 'Gateway to the South' in a Peter Sellers sketch, was first referenced as *Baelgenham* in a Saxon charter of 957. From then until the 18th century, it was little more than a hamlet surrounded by farmland, until villa development crept along the main road from Clapham, earlier than in many London suburbs, which depended on the coming of the railways. It's now a relatively affluent district, packed with shops, bars and restaurants.

The church of **St Mary and St John the Divine** was built as a chapel in 1808 by a dozen of the new, wealthy citizens of Balham, including William Wilberforce and other members of the reforming Clapham Sect. It was considerably altered over time, with the original Greek Revival façade replaced by a Classical one with porches, a domed baptistery and a clocktower.

Large areas of 18th-century Balham were owned by the Duke of Bedford, who sold it on to the wealthy merchant and MP Richardson Borradaile. He laid out **Bedford Hill** as a driveway to reach Bedford Hill House (built in 1802; it was located where Veronica Road now is). The house was demolished in 1897 to make way for the Heaver Estate.

The Priory at 225 Bedford Hill is a white, battlemented Gothic Revival villa from c1810-20. In 1876, it became notorious as the location for the unresolved murder of lawyer Charles Bravo, who was poisoned with antimony. The trial of his wife Florence was a Victorian sensation.

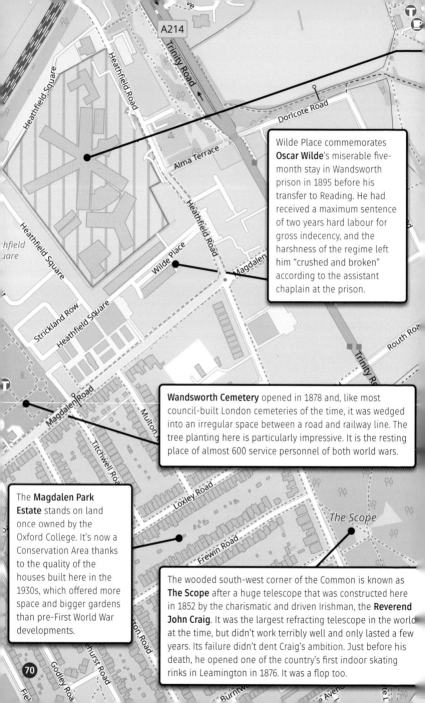

A214

Trinity Road

Heathfield Square

Heathfield Road

Dorlcote Road

Alma Terrace

Heathfield Road

Heathfield Square

hfield uare

Heathfield Square

Wilde Place

Magdalen

Strickland Row

Routh Roa

Trinity Ro

Magdalen Road

Multon

Titchwell Road

Loxley Road

The Scope

Frewin Road

on Road

Godley Roa

Fie

Burntwo

Ave

Wilde Place commemorates **Oscar Wilde**'s miserable five-month stay in Wandsworth prison in 1895 before his transfer to Reading. He had received a maximum sentence of two years hard labour for gross indecency, and the harshness of the regime left him "crushed and broken" according to the assistant chaplain at the prison.

Wandsworth Cemetery opened in 1878 and, like most council-built London cemeteries of the time, it was wedged into an irregular space between a road and railway line. The tree planting here is particularly impressive. It is the resting place of almost 600 service personnel of both world wars.

The **Magdalen Park Estate** stands on land once owned by the Oxford College. It's now a Conservation Area thanks to the quality of the houses built here in the 1930s, which offered more space and bigger gardens than pre-First World War developments.

The wooded south-west corner of the Common is known as **The Scope** after a huge telescope that was constructed here in 1852 by the charismatic and driven Irishman, the **Reverend John Craig**. It was the largest refracting telescope in the world at the time, but didn't work terribly well and only lasted a few years. Its failure didn't dent Craig's ambition. Just before his death, he opened one of the country's first indoor skating rinks in Leamington in 1876. It was a flop too.

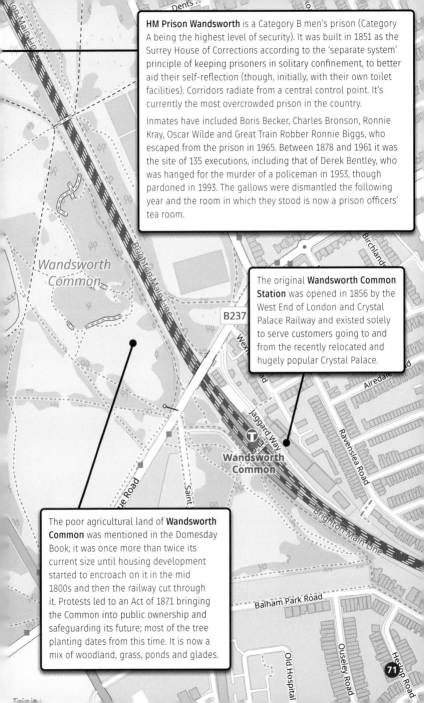

HM Prison Wandsworth is a Category B men's prison (Category A being the highest level of security). It was built in 1851 as the Surrey House of Corrections according to the 'separate system' principle of keeping prisoners in solitary confinement, to better aid their self-reflection (though, initially, with their own toilet facilities). Corridors radiate from a central control point. It's currently the most overcrowded prison in the country.

Inmates have included Boris Becker, Charles Bronson, Ronnie Kray, Oscar Wilde and Great Train Robber Ronnie Biggs, who escaped from the prison in 1965. Between 1878 and 1961 it was the site of 135 executions, including that of Derek Bentley, who was hanged for the murder of a policeman in 1953, though pardoned in 1993. The gallows were dismantled the following year and the room in which they stood is now a prison officers' tea room.

The original **Wandsworth Common Station** was opened in 1856 by the West End of London and Crystal Palace Railway and existed solely to serve customers going to and from the recently relocated and hugely popular Crystal Palace.

The poor agricultural land of **Wandsworth Common** was mentioned in the Domesday Book; it was once more than twice its current size until housing development started to encroach on it in the mid 1800s and then the railway cut through it. Protests led to an Act of 1871 bringing the Common into public ownership and safeguarding its future; most of the tree planting dates from this time. It is now a mix of woodland, grass, ponds and glades.

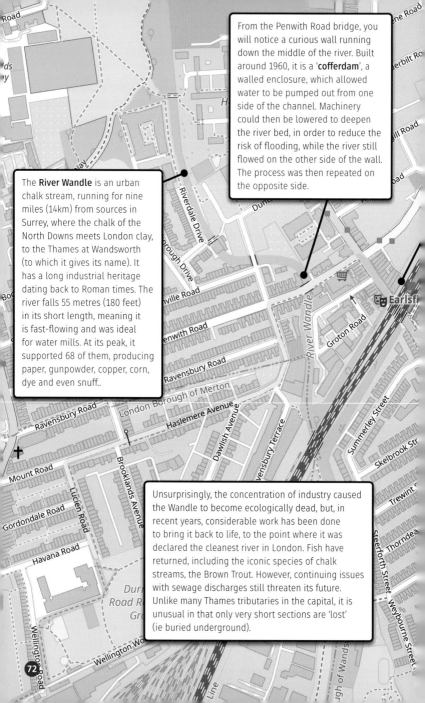

From the Penwith Road bridge, you will notice a curious wall running down the middle of the river. Built around 1960, it is a '**cofferdam**', a walled enclosure, which allowed water to be pumped out from one side of the channel. Machinery could then be lowered to deepen the river bed, in order to reduce the risk of flooding, while the river still flowed on the other side of the wall. The process was then repeated on the opposite side.

The **River Wandle** is an urban chalk stream, running for nine miles (14km) from sources in Surrey, where the chalk of the North Downs meets London clay, to the Thames at Wandsworth (to which it gives its name). It has a long industrial heritage dating back to Roman times. The river falls 55 metres (180 feet) in its short length, meaning it is fast-flowing and was ideal for water mills. At its peak, it supported 68 of them, producing paper, gunpowder, copper, corn, dye and even snuff..

Unsurprisingly, the concentration of industry caused the Wandle to become ecologically dead, but, in recent years, considerable work has been done to bring it back to life, to the point where it was declared the cleanest river in London. Fish have returned, including the iconic species of chalk streams, the Brown Trout. However, continuing issues with sewage discharges still threaten its future. Unlike many Thames tributaries in the capital, it is unusual in that only very short sections are 'lost' (ie buried underground).

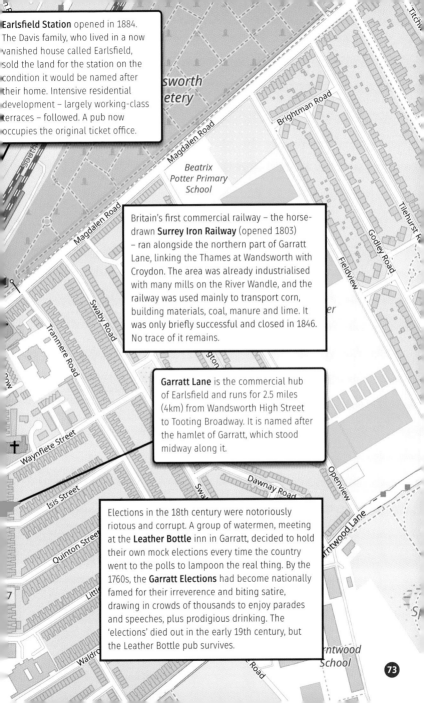

Earlsfield Station opened in 1884. The Davis family, who lived in a now vanished house called Earlsfield, sold the land for the station on the condition it would be named after their home. Intensive residential development – largely working-class terraces – followed. A pub now occupies the original ticket office.

Britain's first commercial railway – the horse-drawn **Surrey Iron Railway** (opened 1803) – ran alongside the northern part of Garratt Lane, linking the Thames at Wandsworth with Croydon. The area was already industrialised with many mills on the River Wandle, and the railway was used mainly to transport corn, building materials, coal, manure and lime. It was only briefly successful and closed in 1846. No trace of it remains.

Garratt Lane is the commercial hub of Earlsfield and runs for 2.5 miles (4km) from Wandsworth High Street to Tooting Broadway. It is named after the hamlet of Garratt, which stood midway along it.

Elections in the 18th century were notoriously riotous and corrupt. A group of watermen, meeting at the **Leather Bottle** inn in Garratt, decided to hold their own mock elections every time the country went to the polls to lampoon the real thing. By the 1760s, the **Garratt Elections** had become nationally famed for their irreverence and biting satire, drawing in crowds of thousands to enjoy parades and speeches, plus prodigious drinking. The 'elections' died out in the early 19th century, but the Leather Bottle pub survives.

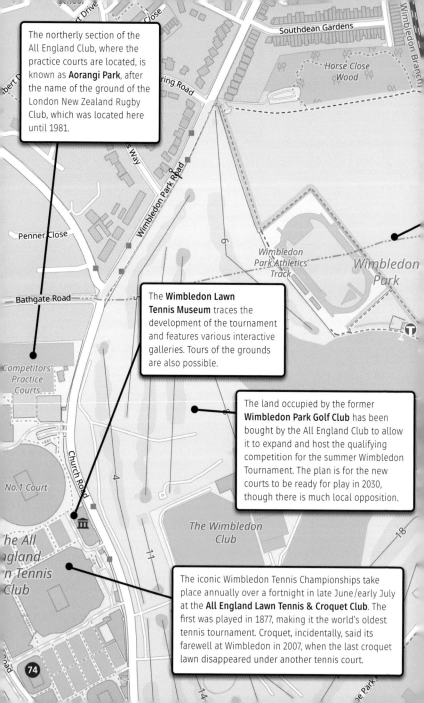

The northerly section of the All England Club, where the practice courts are located, is known as **Aorangi Park**, after the name of the ground of the London New Zealand Rugby Club, which was located here until 1981.

The **Wimbledon Lawn Tennis Museum** traces the development of the tournament and features various interactive galleries. Tours of the grounds are also possible.

The land occupied by the former **Wimbledon Park Golf Club** has been bought by the All England Club to allow it to expand and host the qualifying competition for the summer Wimbledon Tournament. The plan is for the new courts to be ready for play in 2030, though there is much local opposition.

The iconic Wimbledon Tennis Championships take place annually over a fortnight in late June/early July at the **All England Lawn Tennis & Croquet Club**. The first was played in 1877, making it the world's oldest tennis tournament. Croquet, incidentally, said its farewell at Wimbledon in 2007, when the last croquet lawn disappeared under another tennis court.

Southdean Gardens

Horse Close Wood

Wimbledon Park Athletics Track

Wimbledon Park

Penner Close

Bathgate Road

Competitors' Practice Courts

No.1 Court

Church Road

The Wimbledon Club

The All England Lawn Tennis Club

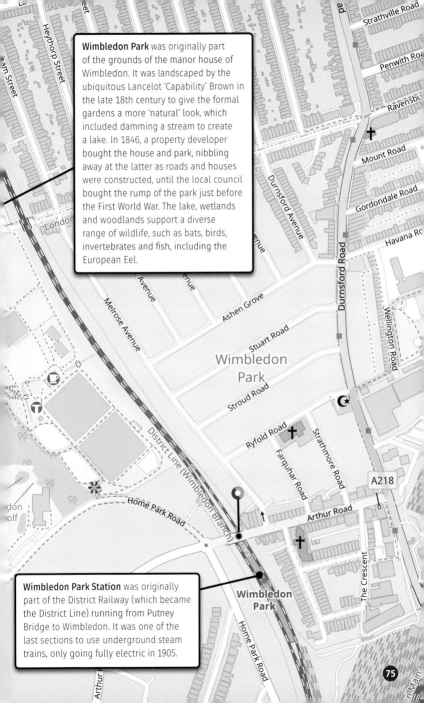

Wimbledon Park was originally part of the grounds of the manor house of Wimbledon. It was landscaped by the ubiquitous Lancelot 'Capability' Brown in the late 18th century to give the formal gardens a more 'natural' look, which included damming a stream to create a lake. In 1846, a property developer bought the house and park, nibbling away at the latter as roads and houses were constructed, until the local council bought the rump of the park just before the First World War. The lake, wetlands and woodlands support a diverse range of wildlife, such as bats, birds, invertebrates and fish, including the European Eel.

Wimbledon Park Station was originally part of the District Railway (which became the District Line) running from Putney Bridge to Wimbledon. It was one of the last sections to use underground steam trains, only going fully electric in 1905.

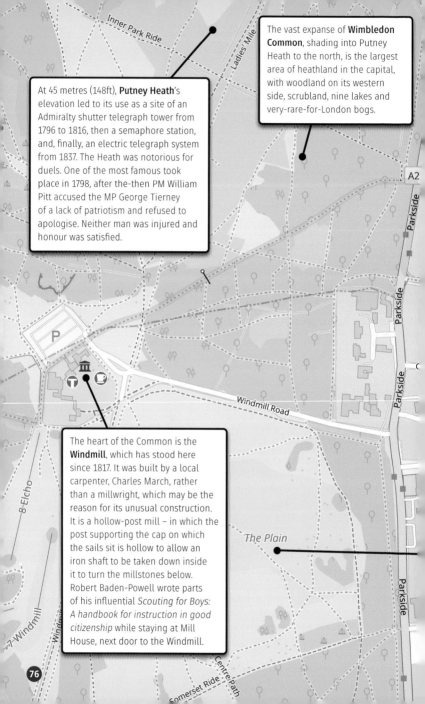

At 45 metres (148ft), **Putney Heath**'s elevation led to its use as a site of an Admiralty shutter telegraph tower from 1796 to 1816, then a semaphore station, and, finally, an electric telegraph system from 1837. The Heath was notorious for duels. One of the most famous took place in 1798, after the-then PM William Pitt accused the MP George Tierney of a lack of patriotism and refused to apologise. Neither man was injured and honour was satisfied.

The vast expanse of **Wimbledon Common**, shading into Putney Heath to the north, is the largest area of heathland in the capital, with woodland on its western side, scrubland, nine lakes and very-rare-for-London bogs.

The heart of the Common is the **Windmill**, which has stood here since 1817. It was built by a local carpenter, Charles March, rather than a millwright, which may be the reason for its unusual construction. It is a hollow-post mill – in which the post supporting the cap on which the sails sit is hollow to allow an iron shaft to be taken down inside it to turn the millstones below. Robert Baden-Powell wrote parts of his influential *Scouting for Boys: A handbook for instruction in good citizenship* while staying at Mill House, next door to the Windmill.

The Common is a particularly valuable habitat for the nationally rare **Stag Beetle**. The beetles emerge above ground from their four to seven-year larval stage from mid May, with the males (with huge 'antlers') often flying around looking for a mate while the smaller females crawl about searching for somewhere to lay their eggs.

Writer Elisabeth Beresford came up with the idea for cuddly eco warriors **The Wombles** when her daughter mispronounced the name of the Common when out for a walk one day. Based on members of her family and named after places with meaning to her, they first appeared in book form in 1968, keeping the Common tidy and living by their slogan to 'make good use of bad rubbish', inspired by Beresford's wartime experience of 'make do and mend'. It was the 1970s animated series, voiced by Bernard Cribbins, and with a classic theme tune by Mike Batt, though, that immortalised them for a generation of children.

The imposing grey bulk of **Queensmere House** was once part of the University of Roehampton's Southlands College, but was converted to luxury flats in the 1990s.

The **Plain** is the largest of four areas of acid grassland on the Common. Eighty plant species have been found here, such as Tormentil, and, in late summer, it is awash in a mosaic of flowering grasses like Yorkshire Fog and Velvet Bent.

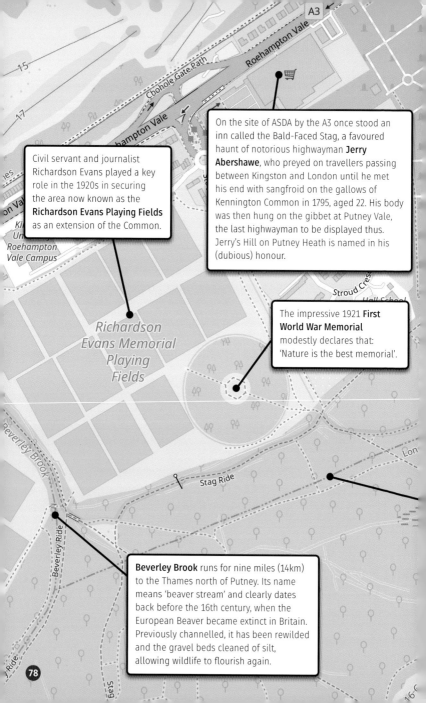

Civil servant and journalist Richardson Evans played a key role in the 1920s in securing the area now known as the **Richardson Evans Playing Fields** as an extension of the Common.

On the site of ASDA by the A3 once stood an inn called the Bald-Faced Stag, a favoured haunt of notorious highwayman **Jerry Abershawe**, who preyed on travellers passing between Kingston and London until he met his end with sangfroid on the gallows of Kennington Common in 1795, aged 22. His body was then hung on the gibbet at Putney Vale, the last highwayman to be displayed thus. Jerry's Hill on Putney Heath is named in his (dubious) honour.

The impressive 1921 **First World War Memorial** modestly declares that: 'Nature is the best memorial'.

Beverley Brook runs for nine miles (14km) to the Thames north of Putney. Its name means 'beaver stream' and clearly dates back before the 16th century, when the European Beaver became extinct in Britain. Previously channelled, it has been rewilded and the gravel beds cleaned of silt, allowing wildlife to flourish again.

Richardson Evans Memorial Playing Fields

Queensmere, surrounded by mature trees, is by far the deepest of the Common's lakes. It supports a thriving fish population, and Yellow and White Water-lilies float on its surface. The lake was created in 1897 to commemorate Queen Victoria's Diamond Jubilee.

Putney Vale Cemetery was laid out on farmland in 1891. Graves include those of film director David Lean, archaeologist Howard Carter and Eugen Sandow, the German bodybuilder, circus strongman and fitness pioneer, who was appointed as special instructor in physical culture to King George V in 1911.

Putney ? Cemetery

Central Drive

Queensmere

London Borough of Wandsworth

12-Queen's Mere

13-Sand Pit

h of Merton

The Ravine

8-Elcho

9-Big Ravine

7-Windmill

Stag Bog is a surviving remnant of one of four rare mires on the Common but all are threatened by the drying out of the boglands and invasive species. The biggest, **Farm Bog**, just south of here has shrunk by 60% since the 1950s, reflecting the decline of peatland habitats across England, and the loss of the species that depend on them. Rarities like Bog Bean and the carnivorous Common Butterwort are just about clinging on here, and will hopefully be saved by plans to restore the mires.

15-Birches

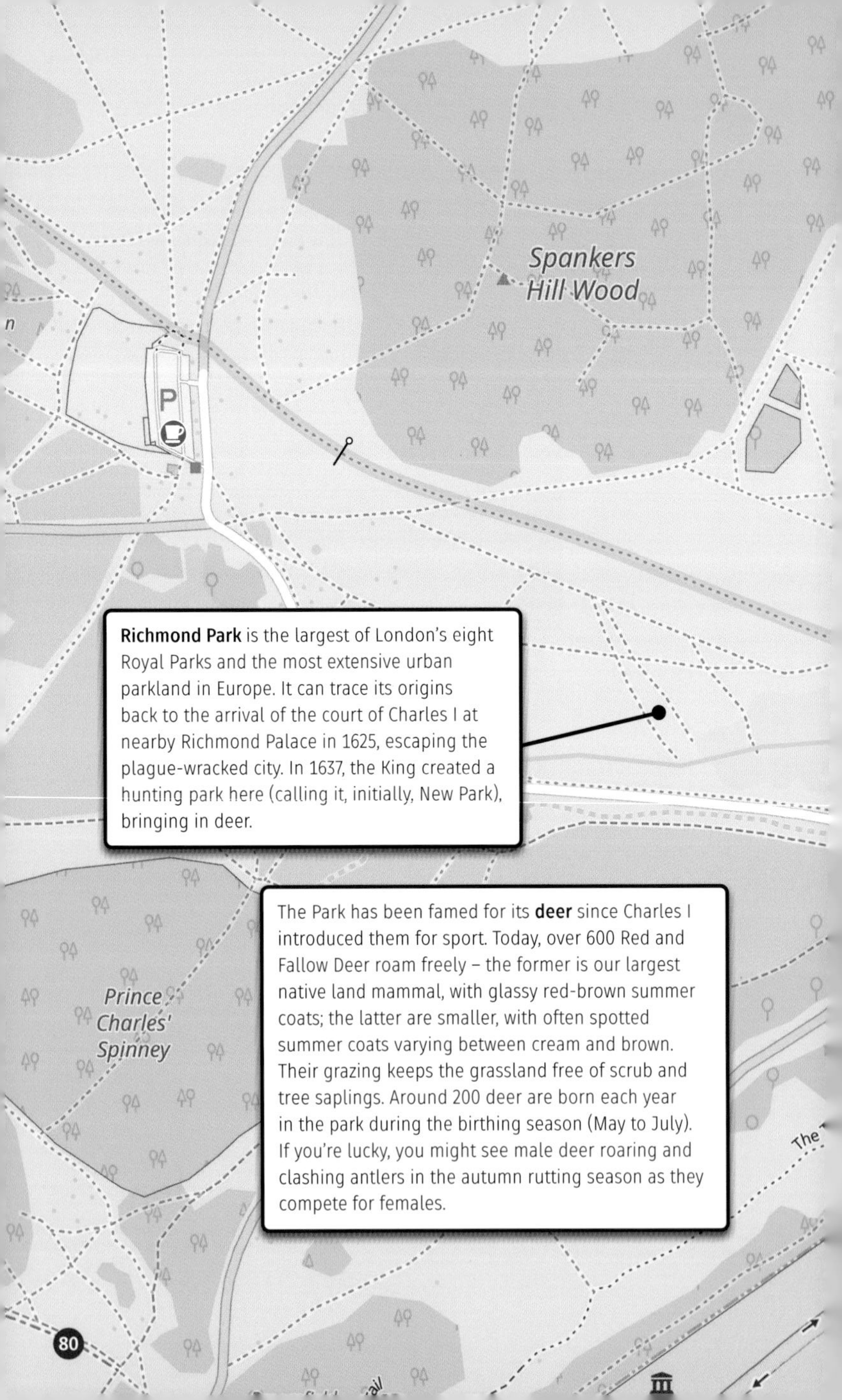

Spankers
Hill Wood

Richmond Park is the largest of London's eight Royal Parks and the most extensive urban parkland in Europe. It can trace its origins back to the arrival of the court of Charles I at nearby Richmond Palace in 1625, escaping the plague-wracked city. In 1637, the King created a hunting park here (calling it, initially, New Park), bringing in deer.

Prince Charles' Spinney

The Park has been famed for its **deer** since Charles I introduced them for sport. Today, over 600 Red and Fallow Deer roam freely – the former is our largest native land mammal, with glassy red-brown summer coats; the latter are smaller, with often spotted summer coats varying between cream and brown. Their grazing keeps the grassland free of scrub and tree saplings. Around 200 deer are born each year in the park during the birthing season (May to July). If you're lucky, you might see male deer roaring and clashing antlers in the autumn rutting season as they compete for females.

The

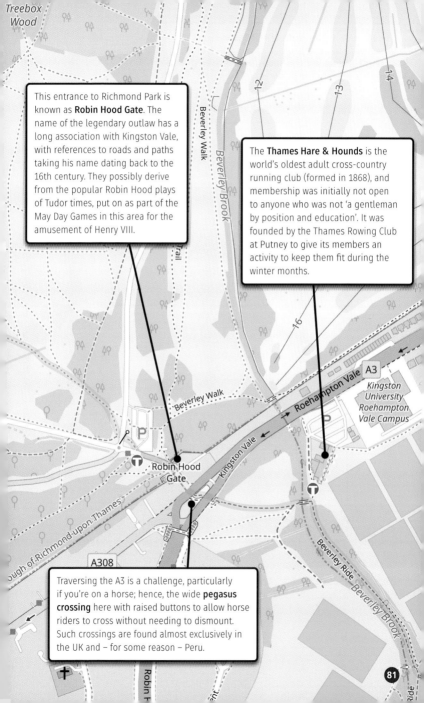

This entrance to Richmond Park is known as **Robin Hood Gate**. The name of the legendary outlaw has a long association with Kingston Vale, with references to roads and paths taking his name dating back to the 16th century. They possibly derive from the popular Robin Hood plays of Tudor times, put on as part of the May Day Games in this area for the amusement of Henry VIII.

The **Thames Hare & Hounds** is the world's oldest adult cross-country running club (formed in 1868), and membership was initially not open to anyone who was not 'a gentleman by position and education'. It was founded by the Thames Rowing Club at Putney to give its members an activity to keep them fit during the winter months.

Traversing the A3 is a challenge, particularly if you're on a horse; hence, the wide **pegasus crossing** here with raised buttons to allow horse riders to cross without needing to dismount. Such crossings are found almost exclusively in the UK and – for some reason – Peru.

Treebox Wood

Beverley Walk

Beverley Brook

Roehampton Vale A3

Kingston University Roehampton Vale Campus

Beverley Walk

Kingston Vale

Robin Hood Gate

ough of Richmond-upon-Thames

Beverley Ride – Beverley Brook

A308

Robin H

There are more than a dozen **woods** and **plantations** all over the Park. Many of the latter date from the early 19th century, when former Prime Minister Viscount Sidmouth was Deputy Ranger. The trees were selected for their usefulness in shipbuilding (such as Oak) or for providing sizeable seeds (like Horse Chestnut) upon which the deer could feed. Sidmouth Wood bears his name and is now particularly rich in birdlife.

Way

Sidmouth Wood

Queen Elizabeth's Plantation

When Charles I established the Park, he enclosed it with walls (many of which still stand), much to the dismay of the locals, though he did allow restricted access. By the mid 18th century, even this was in danger by George II's daughter Amelia, who was living at White Lodge as Ranger of the Park and tried to keep out anyone without a specially issued ticket. However, a mass trespass followed and, eventually, an outraged Richmond brewer, **John Lewis**, brought a case to court in 1758, which re-established public access. It has never been threatened since, though the Park only became fully open to the public in 1904.

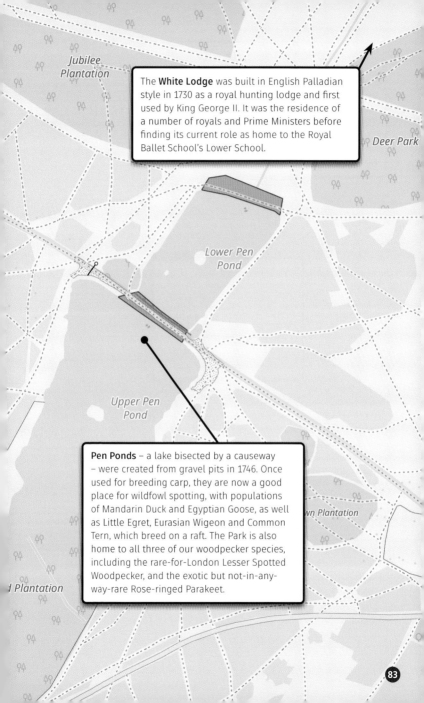

The **White Lodge** was built in English Palladian style in 1730 as a royal hunting lodge and first used by King George II. It was the residence of a number of royals and Prime Ministers before finding its current role as home to the Royal Ballet School's Lower School.

Jubilee Plantation

Deer Park

Lower Pen Pond

Upper Pen Pond

wn Plantation

l Plantation

Pen Ponds – a lake bisected by a causeway – were created from gravel pits in 1746. Once used for breeding carp, they are now a good place for wildfowl spotting, with populations of Mandarin Duck and Egyptian Goose, as well as Little Egret, Eurasian Wigeon and Common Tern, which breed on a raft. The Park is also home to all three of our woodpecker species, including the rare-for-London Lesser Spotted Woodpecker, and the exotic but not-in-any-way-rare Rose-ringed Parakeet.

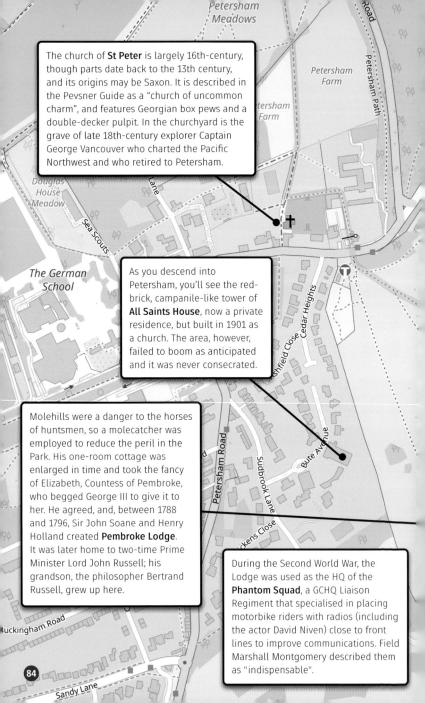

The church of **St Peter** is largely 16th-century, though parts date back to the 13th century, and its origins may be Saxon. It is described in the Pevsner Guide as a "church of uncommon charm", and features Georgian box pews and a double-decker pulpit. In the churchyard is the grave of late 18th-century explorer Captain George Vancouver who charted the Pacific Northwest and who retired to Petersham.

As you descend into Petersham, you'll see the red-brick, campanile-like tower of **All Saints House**, now a private residence, but built in 1901 as a church. The area, however, failed to boom as anticipated and it was never consecrated.

Molehills were a danger to the horses of huntsmen, so a molecatcher was employed to reduce the peril in the Park. His one-room cottage was enlarged in time and took the fancy of Elizabeth, Countess of Pembroke, who begged George III to give it to her. He agreed, and, between 1788 and 1796, Sir John Soane and Henry Holland created **Pembroke Lodge**. It was later home to two-time Prime Minister Lord John Russell; his grandson, the philosopher Bertrand Russell, grew up here.

During the Second World War, the Lodge was used as the HQ of the **Phantom Squad**, a GCHQ Liaison Regiment that specialised in placing motorbike riders with radios (including the actor David Niven) close to front lines to improve communications. Field Marshall Montgomery described them as "indispensable".

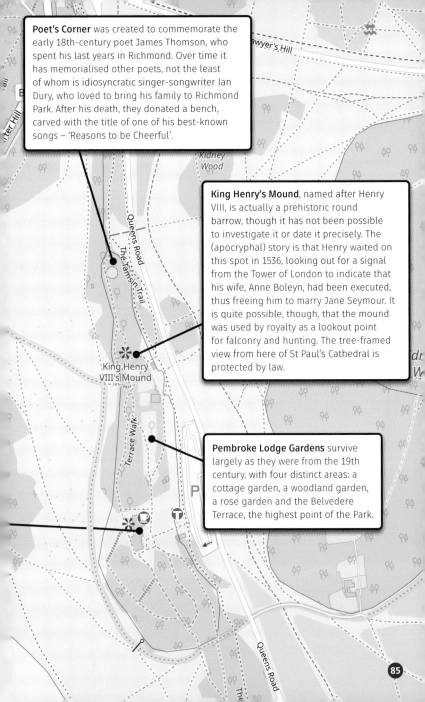

Poet's Corner was created to commemorate the early 18th-century poet James Thomson, who spent his last years in Richmond. Over time it has memorialised other poets, not the least of whom is idiosyncratic singer-songwriter Ian Dury, who loved to bring his family to Richmond Park. After his death, they donated a bench, carved with the title of one of his best-known songs – 'Reasons to be Cheerful'.

King Henry's Mound, named after Henry VIII, is actually a prehistoric round barrow, though it has not been possible to investigate it or date it precisely. The (apocryphal) story is that Henry waited on this spot in 1536, looking out for a signal from the Tower of London to indicate that his wife, Anne Boleyn, had been executed, thus freeing him to marry Jane Seymour. It is quite possible, though, that the mound was used by royalty as a lookout point for falconry and hunting. The tree-framed view from here of St Paul's Cathedral is protected by law.

Pembroke Lodge Gardens survive largely as they were from the 19th century, with four distinct areas: a cottage garden, a woodland garden, a rose garden and the Belvedere Terrace, the highest point of the Park.

Sawyer's Hill

Kidney Wood

Queens Road

The Tamsin Trail

King Henry VIII's Mound

Terrace Walk

Queens Road

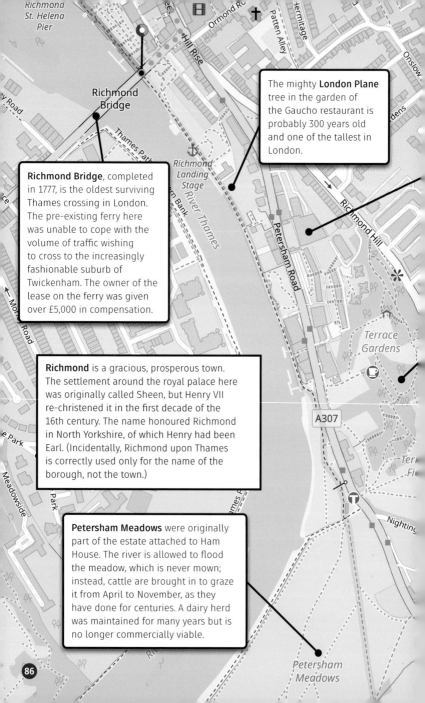

The mighty **London Plane** tree in the garden of the Gaucho restaurant is probably 300 years old and one of the tallest in London.

Richmond Bridge, completed in 1777, is the oldest surviving Thames crossing in London. The pre-existing ferry here was unable to cope with the volume of traffic wishing to cross to the increasingly fashionable suburb of Twickenham. The owner of the lease on the ferry was given over £5,000 in compensation.

Richmond is a gracious, prosperous town. The settlement around the royal palace here was originally called Sheen, but Henry VII re-christened it in the first decade of the 16th century. The name honoured Richmond in North Yorkshire, of which Henry had been Earl. (Incidentally, Richmond upon Thames is correctly used only for the name of the borough, not the town.)

Petersham Meadows were originally part of the estate attached to Ham House. The river is allowed to flood the meadow, which is never mown; instead, cattle are brought in to graze it from April to November, as they have done for centuries. A dairy herd was maintained for many years but is no longer commercially viable.

The **Poppy Factory** was founded in 1922 by Major George Howson to offer employment to disabled servicemen in creating artificial poppies. (The poppy had been adopted the previous year by the British Legion as a symbol of remembrance.) He wasn't optimistic for the venture: "I do not think it can be a great success, but it is worth trying." It was an instant success, producing 30 million poppies a year by 1931; it continues to help veterans with health conditions move towards employment today, and to produce over six million poppies annually. The current Art Deco-style building dates from 1933.

The **Terrace Gardens** and **Buccleuch Gardens** (linked by a tunnel under the main road) were laid out in the 18th century as the private gardens of three grand houses. They were opened as a public park in 1887, with the gardens of further mansion being added in the 1920s. None of the houses survive, but the gardens maintain much of their 19th-century layout.

Wick House was built for the painter Sir Joshua Reynolds by architect Sir William Chambers in 1772 as an out-of-town getaway for entertaining friends.

The **Petersham Hotel** was built in Italian Gothic style in 1865 by John Giles, who also created the Langham Hotel in Portland Place.

High on Richmond Hill, sits the **Royal Star and Garter Home**, which opened in 1924. It was built on the site of a hotel (where Dickens was a frequent visitor) to provide for up to 180 injured servicemen. In 1948, residents took part in a forerunner of the Paralympic Games, organised by neurologist Dr Ludwig Guttmann, a seminal figure in the history of paralympic athletics. In 2013, it was sold and is now private apartments.

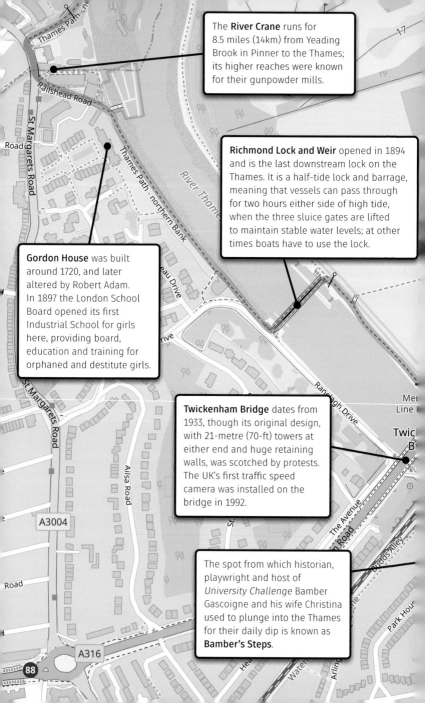

The **River Crane** runs for 8.5 miles (14km) from Yeading Brook in Pinner to the Thames; its higher reaches were known for their gunpowder mills.

Richmond Lock and Weir opened in 1894 and is the last downstream lock on the Thames. It is a half-tide lock and barrage, meaning that vessels can pass through for two hours either side of high tide, when the three sluice gates are lifted to maintain stable water levels; at other times boats have to use the lock.

Gordon House was built around 1720, and later altered by Robert Adam. In 1897 the London School Board opened its first Industrial School for girls here, providing board, education and training for orphaned and destitute girls.

Twickenham Bridge dates from 1933, though its original design, with 21-metre (70-ft) towers at either end and huge retaining walls, was scotched by protests. The UK's first traffic speed camera was installed on the bridge in 1992.

The spot from which historian, playwright and host of *University Challenge* Bamber Gascoigne and his wife Christina used to plunge into the Thames for their daily dip is known as **Bamber's Steps**.

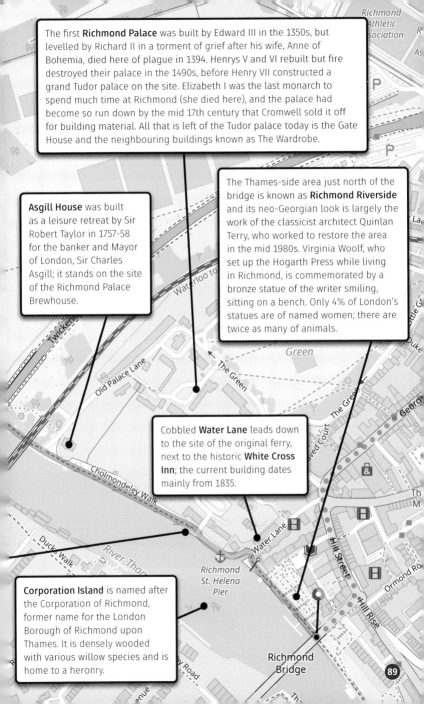

The first **Richmond Palace** was built by Edward III in the 1350s, but levelled by Richard II in a torment of grief after his wife, Anne of Bohemia, died here of plague in 1394. Henrys V and VI rebuilt but fire destroyed their palace in the 1490s, before Henry VII constructed a grand Tudor palace on the site. Elizabeth I was the last monarch to spend much time at Richmond (she died here), and the palace had become so run down by the mid 17th century that Cromwell sold it off for building material. All that is left of the Tudor palace today is the Gate House and the neighbouring buildings known as The Wardrobe.

The Thames-side area just north of the bridge is known as **Richmond Riverside** and its neo-Georgian look is largely the work of the classicist architect Quinlan Terry, who worked to restore the area in the mid 1980s. Virginia Woolf, who set up the Hogarth Press while living in Richmond, is commemorated by a bronze statue of the writer smiling, sitting on a bench. Only 4% of London's statues are of named women; there are twice as many of animals.

Asgill House was built as a leisure retreat by Sir Robert Taylor in 1757-58 for the banker and Mayor of London, Sir Charles Asgill; it stands on the site of the Richmond Palace Brewhouse.

Cobbled **Water Lane** leads down to the site of the original ferry, next to the historic **White Cross Inn**; the current building dates mainly from 1835.

Corporation Island is named after the Corporation of Richmond, former name for the London Borough of Richmond upon Thames. It is densely wooded with various willow species and is home to a heronry.

A ferry used to run across the river from **Isleworth Stairs** to the Old Deer Park. This is the spot from which Catherine Howard sailed down the Thames to her execution in the Tower of London in 1542. Eleven years later, Lady Jane Grey embarked from the same place for the same destination. She had anticipated being crowned monarch following the death of Edward VI, but the 'Nine Days' Queen' ended up suffering the same fate as Catherine in 1554.

The **London Apprentice** pub dates from the early 18th century, though there has been an inn on the site since Tudor times. Its name may be drawn from a popular 17th-century ballad 'The Honour of an Apprentice of London' or from the apprentices of the city livery companies, who would row up the river to the pub on their days off. Everyone from Henry VIII to Dick Turpin has been claimed as a former patron.

The **Duke of Northumberland's River** is an artificial watercourse (dug in Tudor times by 80 specialist 'ditchers'). It was created to power mills that produced flour and calico. The Dukes of Northumberland have owned nearby Syon House since the 18th century.

Isleworth is first mentioned in an Anglo-Saxon charter of 695 with the tongue-twisting name of *Gislheresuuyrth*, meaning 'enclosure belonging to Gislhere'. By the time of the Domesday Book, it was a prosperous trading and farming community. By the 18th and 19th centuries, orchards and market gardens dominated, as did fine villas and mansions.

An '**ait**' or '**eyot**' is the name for a river island, commonly used for those in the Thames. Aits are usually long and thin, built on an accumulation of sediment; tidal erosion causes their shape to constantly shift. The name derives from the Old English *iggath* or *igeth*, meaning 'island'.

St. Mary's Catholic Primary School

Isleworth

A310

South Street

Silverhall Park

North Street

Mill Plat

Mill Plat Avenue

Tolson Road

Byfield Road

Clock Tower Road

Redlees Park

Brantwood

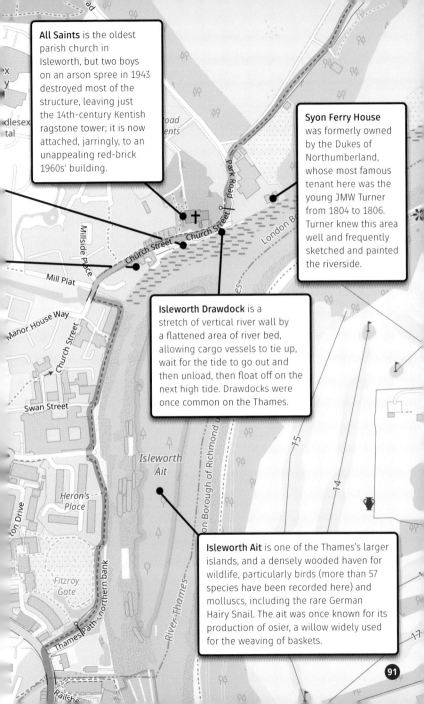

All Saints is the oldest parish church in Isleworth, but two boys on an arson spree in 1943 destroyed most of the structure, leaving just the 14th-century Kentish ragstone tower; it is now attached, jarringly, to an unappealing red-brick 1960s' building.

Syon Ferry House was formerly owned by the Dukes of Northumberland, whose most famous tenant here was the young JMW Turner from 1804 to 1806. Turner knew this area well and frequently sketched and painted the riverside.

Isleworth Drawdock is a stretch of vertical river wall by a flattened area of river bed, allowing cargo vessels to tie up, wait for the tide to go out and then unload, then float off on the next high tide. Drawdocks were once common on the Thames.

Isleworth Ait is one of the Thames's larger islands, and a densely wooded haven for wildlife, particularly birds (more than 57 species have been recorded here) and molluscs, including the rare German Hairy Snail. The ait was once known for its production of osier, a willow widely used for the weaving of baskets.

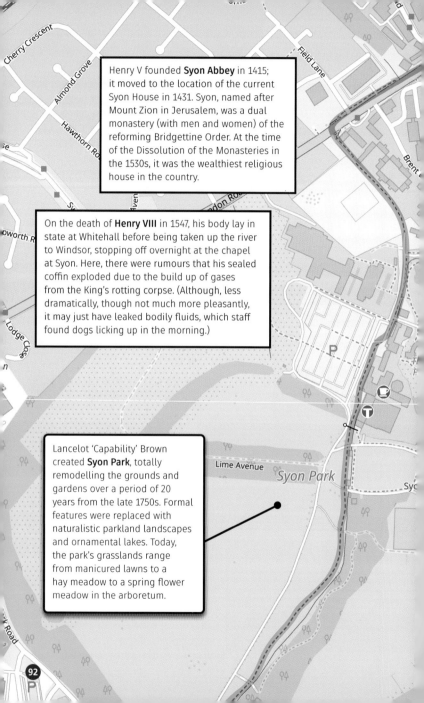

Henry V founded **Syon Abbey** in 1415; it moved to the location of the current Syon House in 1431. Syon, named after Mount Zion in Jerusalem, was a dual monastery (with men and women) of the reforming Bridgettine Order. At the time of the Dissolution of the Monasteries in the 1530s, it was the wealthiest religious house in the country.

On the death of **Henry VIII** in 1547, his body lay in state at Whitehall before being taken up the river to Windsor, stopping off overnight at the chapel at Syon. Here, there were rumours that his sealed coffin exploded due to the build up of gases from the King's rotting corpse. (Although, less dramatically, though not much more pleasantly, it may just have leaked bodily fluids, which staff found dogs licking up in the morning.)

Lancelot 'Capability' Brown created **Syon Park**, totally remodelling the grounds and gardens over a period of 20 years from the late 1750s. Formal features were replaced with naturalistic parkland landscapes and ornamental lakes. Today, the park's grasslands range from manicured lawns to a hay meadow to a spring flower meadow in the arboretum.

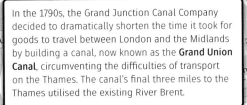

In the 1790s, the Grand Junction Canal Company decided to dramatically shorten the time it took for goods to travel between London and the Midlands by building a canal, now known as the **Grand Union Canal**, circumventing the difficulties of transport on the Thames. The canal's final three miles to the Thames utilised the existing River Brent.

Brentford Dock opened in 1859 and became a major trans-shipment hub between the barges of the Thames and the Great Western Railway. It closed in 1964 and was redeveloped in the early 1970s as a marina and housing.

The elegant **Great Conservatory**, designed by Charles Fowler, was completed in 1827 and was the first large-scale metal-framed glasshouse to be built in the country.

Ecologically, the most important part of Syon Park is the Thames-side **Tide Meadow**. It is the largest area of unbanked riverside on the tidal river, flooding at high tide to create a marshland where tall grasses flourish and wintering birds shelter.

The exterior of **Syon House** remains much as it was in the 16th century, when the remains of the abbey were transformed into a private house; its interiors were extensively remodelled in classical style by Robert Adam in 1762-69. Syon has been in the hands of the Dukes of Northumberland since 1594.

On 26th July 1609, the scientist **Thomas Harriot** created the first detailed drawings of the Moon from his observations through a telescope at Syon House, pre-empting Galileo by several months.

Grand Union Canal

Clitherow's Island

Grand Union Canal towpath

River Brent

Star Estate

Transport Avenue

The iron **Gallows Bridge** was probably designed by Thomas Telford and dates from 1820. Its surface was originally rough to allow canal horses to maintain their grip as they passed over. The origin of its name is uncertain, but might refer to a man found hanged in Boston Manor woods in the 17th century.

Clitheroe's Lock honours, even though misspelling, the Clitherow family of Boston Manor House.

There have been two **Battles of Brentford**. In 1016, the English King Edmund Ironside beat back the invading Danish forces of Cnut on the banks of the Thames, though Edmund's death later that year resulted in the English Crown being given to Cnut. In 1642, the Royalists under Prince Rupert drove a small Parliamentarian force out of Brentford. Their subsequent sacking of the town did much to solidify the support of Londoners for Parliament.

Shield Drive

West Cross Industrial Park

Brentford's least likely resident? None other than **Pocahontas**, she of the helping-the-new-colonists fame in Virginia in the early 17th century. The daughter of the Powhatan tribal chief, she was captured by the newcomers, learned English and ended up marrying tobacco grower John Rolfe before coming to England in 1616 with him to promote the colony. She died the next year in Gravesend, attempting to return to Virginia to escape London's pollution.

Amalgamated Drive

West Cross Way

Great West Road

Grant Way

Gilette Corner

B454

This section of the **Great West Road** (A4) is sometimes, rather misleadingly, known as the 'Golden Mile' due to the concentration of commerce and industry beside the road. Among the early factories to spring up – often in notable Art Deco-inspired buildings – were Hudson-Essex Motors, Smith's Potato Crisps and the Firestone Tyre Company.

Great West Road

Jacobean **Boston Manor House** was built for Lady Mary Reade in 1633. It was owned by the Clitherow family from the 1670s until the 1920s. It is open to the public with rooms restored in a range of 17th, 18th and 19th century styles.

It's not difficult to work out the meaning of **Brentford**: ford across the River Brent. Its location, at the confluence of the Brent and the Thames, was probably why a settlement was built here in pre-Roman times (before the founding of London). The range of Bronze and Iron Age pottery, burnt flints and other artefacts found in the area suggest it might have been a tribal meeting place.

Boston Manor Park was created in 1924 from part of the estate of Boston Manor House, and is a mix of open space and woodland. The estate itself dates back to at least the 12th century, and it remained a green oasis as Brentford urbanised around it until its character was irrevocably changed with the building of the M4 right through the centre of it in the 1960s.

The **Brentford Gauging Lock** was once one of the busiest spots on the canal. At a gauging lock a toll keeper would use a gauging rod to measure the height of a boat out of the water to calculate the weight of cargo it was carrying so he could levy the appropriate toll. The tiny **Toll House** museum is usually open on Fridays.

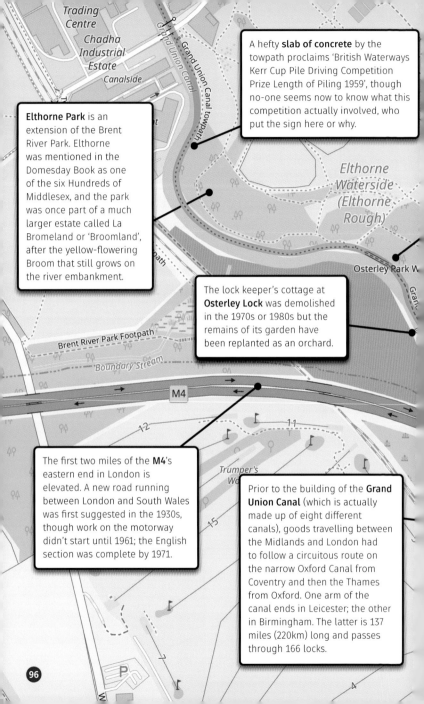

Trading Centre

Chadha Industrial Estate

Canalside

Grand Union Canal

Grand Union Canal towpath

A hefty **slab of concrete** by the towpath proclaims 'British Waterways Kerr Cup Pile Driving Competition Prize Length of Piling 1959', though no-one seems now to know what this competition actually involved, who put the sign here or why.

Elthorne Park is an extension of the Brent River Park. Elthorne was mentioned in the Domesday Book as one of the six Hundreds of Middlesex, and the park was once part of a much larger estate called La Bromeland or 'Broomland', after the yellow-flowering Broom that still grows on the river embankment.

Elthorne Waterside (Elthorne Rough)

Osterley Park W

Gran

The lock keeper's cottage at **Osterley Lock** was demolished in the 1970s or 1980s but the remains of its garden have been replanted as an orchard.

Brent River Park Footpath

Boundary Stream

M4

12

11

Trumper's Wa

The first two miles of the **M4**'s eastern end in London is elevated. A new road running between London and South Wales was first suggested in the 1930s, though work on the motorway didn't start until 1961; the English section was complete by 1971.

15

Prior to the building of the **Grand Union Canal** (which is actually made up of eight different canals), goods travelling between the Midlands and London had to follow a circuitous route on the narrow Oxford Canal from Coventry and then the Thames from Oxford. One arm of the canal ends in Leicester; the other in Birmingham. The latter is 137 miles (220km) long and passes through 166 locks.

P

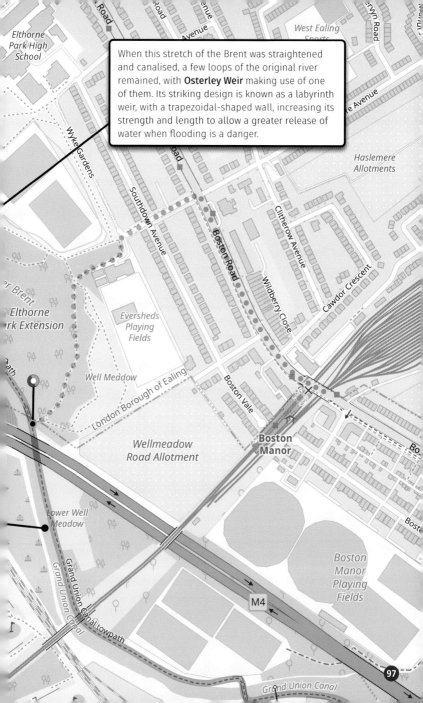

When this stretch of the Brent was straightened and canalised, a few loops of the original river remained, with **Osterley Weir** making use of one of them. Its striking design is known as a labyrinth weir, with a trapezoidal-shaped wall, increasing its strength and length to allow a greater release of water when flooding is a danger.

Elthorne Park High School

West Ealing Sports

Wyke Gardens

Haslemere Allotments

Southdown Avenue

Boston Road

Clitherow Avenue

Cawdor Crescent

er Brent

Elthorne rk Extension

Eversheds Playing Fields

Wildberry Close

Well Meadow

London Borough of Ealing

Boston Vale

Wellmeadow Road Allotment

Boston Manor

Lower Well Meadow

Boston Manor Playing Fields

Grand Union Canal towpath

Grand Union Canal

M4

Grand Union Canal

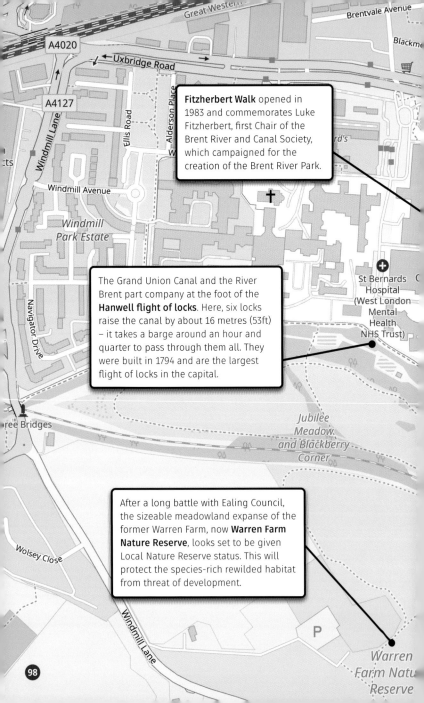

Fitzherbert Walk opened in 1983 and commemorates Luke Fitzherbert, first Chair of the Brent River and Canal Society, which campaigned for the creation of the Brent River Park.

The Grand Union Canal and the River Brent part company at the foot of the **Hanwell flight of locks**. Here, six locks raise the canal by about 16 metres (53ft) – it takes a barge around an hour and quarter to pass through them all. They were built in 1794 and are the largest flight of locks in the capital.

After a long battle with Ealing Council, the sizeable meadowland expanse of the former Warren Farm, now **Warren Farm Nature Reserve**, looks set to be given Local Nature Reserve status. This will protect the species-rich rewilded habitat from threat of development.

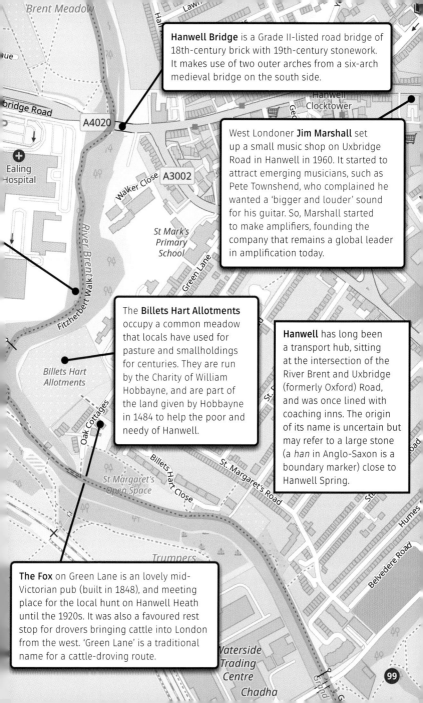

Hanwell Bridge is a Grade II-listed road bridge of 18th-century brick with 19th-century stonework. It makes use of two outer arches from a six-arch medieval bridge on the south side.

West Londoner **Jim Marshall** set up a small music shop on Uxbridge Road in Hanwell in 1960. It started to attract emerging musicians, such as Pete Townshend, who complained he wanted a 'bigger and louder' sound for his guitar. So, Marshall started to make amplifiers, founding the company that remains a global leader in amplification today.

The **Billets Hart Allotments** occupy a common meadow that locals have used for pasture and smallholdings for centuries. They are run by the Charity of William Hobbayne, and are part of the land given by Hobbayne in 1484 to help the poor and needy of Hanwell.

Hanwell has long been a transport hub, sitting at the intersection of the River Brent and Uxbridge (formerly Oxford) Road, and was once lined with coaching inns. The origin of its name is uncertain but may refer to a large stone (a *han* in Anglo-Saxon is a boundary marker) close to Hanwell Spring.

The Fox on Green Lane is an lovely mid-Victorian pub (built in 1848), and meeting place for the local hunt on Hanwell Heath until the 1920s. It was also a favoured rest stop for drovers bringing cattle into London from the west. 'Green Lane' is a traditional name for a cattle-droving route.

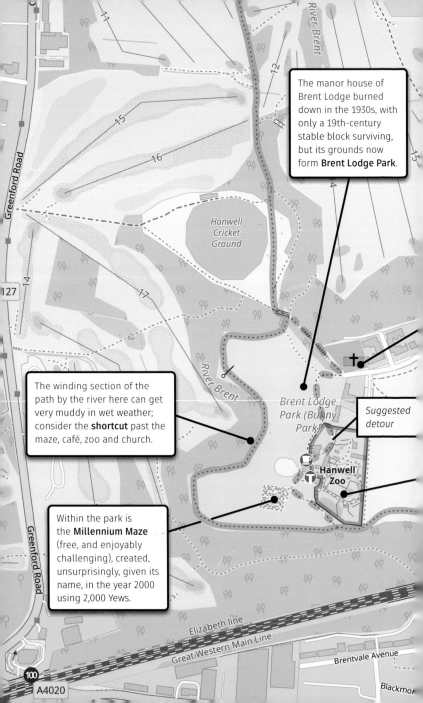

The manor house of Brent Lodge burned down in the 1930s, with only a 19th-century stable block surviving, but its grounds now form **Brent Lodge Park**.

Hanwell Cricket Ground

The winding section of the path by the river here can get very muddy in wet weather; consider the **shortcut** past the maze, café, zoo and church.

Brent Lodge Park (Bunny Park)

Suggested detour

Hanwell Zoo

Within the park is the **Millennium Maze** (free, and enjoyably challenging), created, unsurprisingly, given its name, in the year 2000 using 2,000 Yews.

River Brent

River Brent

Greenford Road

Greenford Road

Elizabeth line

Great Western Main Line

Brentvale Avenue

Blackmor

A4020

127

100

Seven Saxon graves were discovered in 1886, leading to speculation that this could have been the site of the **Battle of Bloody Croft** between the Romano-British and the Saxons, some time around AD 572. Evidence is scant, however, though *wael* means 'slaughter' in Anglo-Saxon, which just possibly could account for the 'well' in Hanwell.

The church of **St Mary** sits at Hanwell's highest point. It dates originally from the 12th century but had become too small for its congregation by the 19th century. George Gilbert Scott was commissioned to build a bigger church in Gothic Revival style, which was consecrated in 1842; it was one of Scott's first churches and he later felt embarrassed by it, describing it as a "mass of horrors". Inside, is a plaque to the boxer Billy Wells, who is better known as the man striking the gong at the start of Rank films.

Hanwell Zoo, known locally as 'Bunny Park', opened in 1975 and majors on birds and small mammals, such as flamingos, meerkats, lemurs and porcupines.

The eight-arched **Wharncliffe Viaduct** is a stunningly incongruous sight . As Pevsner says, "Few viaducts have such architectural panache". It carries the Great Western Main Line and was Isambard Kingdom Brunel's first major structural project. Built in 1836-37, it stands at 270 metres (890ft) long and 20 metres (66ft) high, with unusual hollow (and, therefore, cheaper to build) piers that have been colonised by bats. Lord Wharncliffe chaired the parliamentary committee that took the GWR Bill through Parliament.

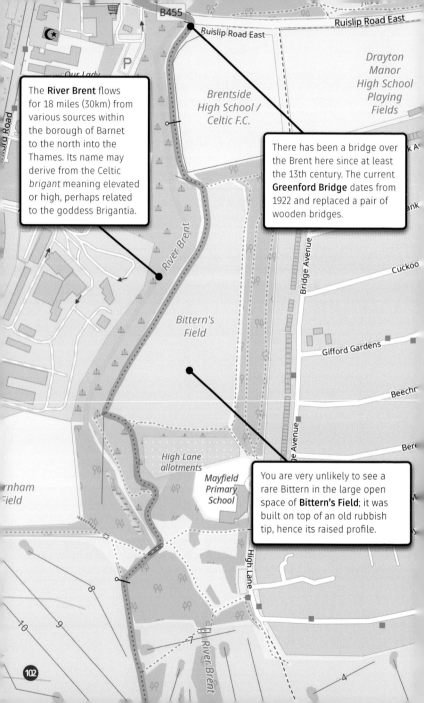

The **River Brent** flows for 18 miles (30km) from various sources within the borough of Barnet to the north into the Thames. Its name may derive from the Celtic *brigant* meaning elevated or high, perhaps related to the goddess Brigantia.

There has been a bridge over the Brent here since at least the 13th century. The current **Greenford Bridge** dates from 1922 and replaced a pair of wooden bridges.

You are very unlikely to see a rare Bittern in the large open space of **Bittern's Field**; it was built on top of an old rubbish tip, hence its raised profile.

B455

Ruislip Road East

Ruislip Road East

Drayton Manor High School Playing Fields

Brentside High School / Celtic F.C.

Our Lady

River Brent

Bridge Avenue

Cuckoo

Bittern's Field

Gifford Gardens

Beechr

e Avenue

Bere

High Lane allotments

Mayfield Primary School

High Lane

rnham Field

River Brent

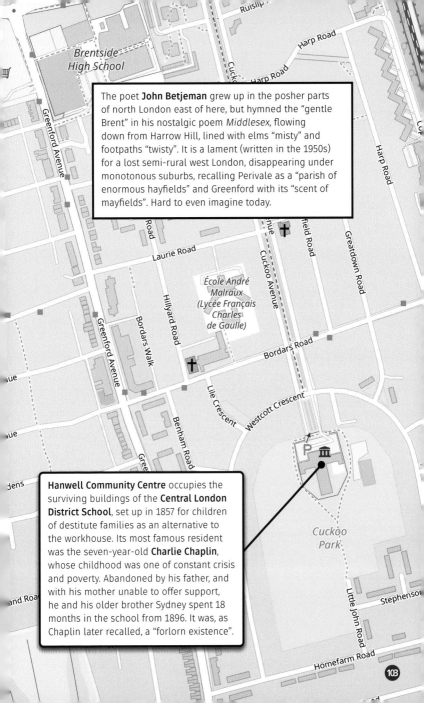

The poet **John Betjeman** grew up in the posher parts of north London east of here, but hymned the "gentle Brent" in his nostalgic poem *Middlesex*, flowing down from Harrow Hill, lined with elms "misty" and footpaths "twisty". It is a lament (written in the 1950s) for a lost semi-rural west London, disappearing under monotonous suburbs, recalling Perivale as a "parish of enormous hayfields" and Greenford with its "scent of mayfields". Hard to even imagine today.

Hanwell Community Centre occupies the surviving buildings of the **Central London District School**, set up in 1857 for children of destitute families as an alternative to the workhouse. Its most famous resident was the seven-year-old **Charlie Chaplin**, whose childhood was one of constant crisis and poverty. Abandoned by his father, and with his mother unable to offer support, he and his older brother Sydney spent 18 months in the school from 1896. It was, as Chaplin later recalled, a "forlorn existence".

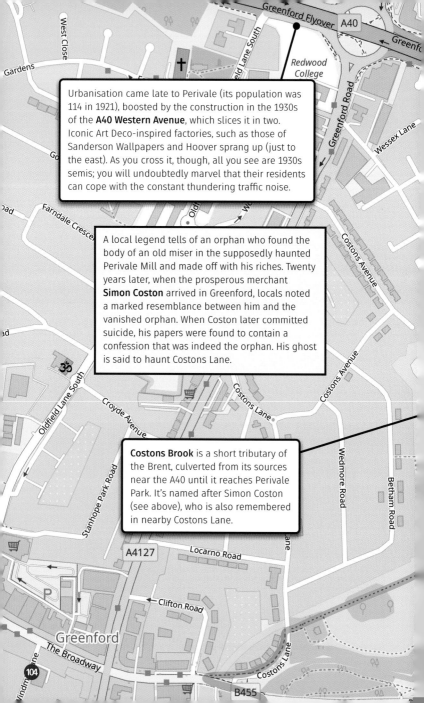

Urbanisation came late to Perivale (its population was 114 in 1921), boosted by the construction in the 1930s of the **A40 Western Avenue**, which slices it in two. Iconic Art Deco-inspired factories, such as those of Sanderson Wallpapers and Hoover sprang up (just to the east). As you cross it, though, all you see are 1930s semis; you will undoubtedly marvel that their residents can cope with the constant thundering traffic noise.

A local legend tells of an orphan who found the body of an old miser in the supposedly haunted Perivale Mill and made off with his riches. Twenty years later, when the prosperous merchant **Simon Coston** arrived in Greenford, locals noted a marked resemblance between him and the vanished orphan. When Coston later committed suicide, his papers were found to contain a confession that was indeed the orphan. His ghost is said to haunt Costons Lane.

Costons Brook is a short tributary of the Brent, culverted from its sources near the A40 until it reaches Perivale Park. It's named after Simon Coston (see above), who is also remembered in nearby Costons Lane.

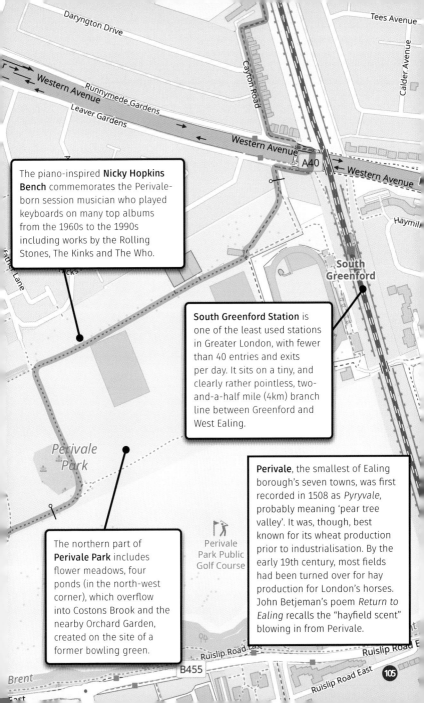

The piano-inspired **Nicky Hopkins Bench** commemorates the Perivale-born session musician who played keyboards on many top albums from the 1960s to the 1990s including works by the Rolling Stones, The Kinks and The Who.

South Greenford Station is one of the least used stations in Greater London, with fewer than 40 entries and exits per day. It sits on a tiny, and clearly rather pointless, two-and-a-half mile (4km) branch line between Greenford and West Ealing.

Perivale, the smallest of Ealing borough's seven towns, was first recorded in 1508 as *Pyryvale*, probably meaning 'pear tree valley'. It was, though, best known for its wheat production prior to industrialisation. By the early 19th century, most fields had been turned over for hay production for London's horses. John Betjeman's poem *Return to Ealing* recalls the "hayfield scent" blowing in from Perivale.

The northern part of **Perivale Park** includes flower meadows, four ponds (in the north-west corner), which overflow into Costons Brook and the nearby Orchard Garden, created on the site of a former bowling green.

Perivale Park Public Golf Course

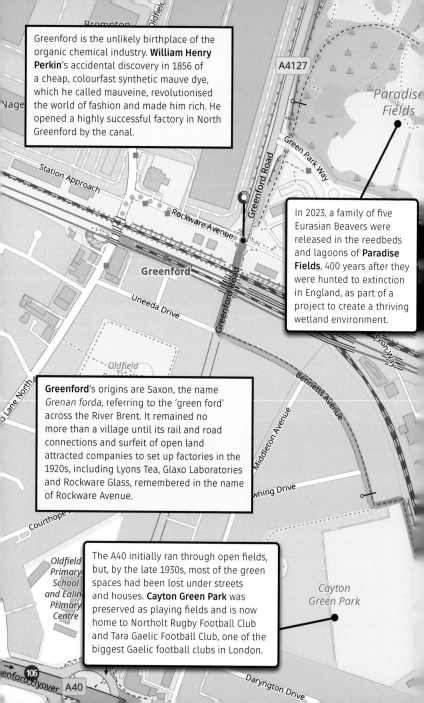

Greenford is the unlikely birthplace of the organic chemical industry. **William Henry Perkin**'s accidental discovery in 1856 of a cheap, colourfast synthetic mauve dye, which he called mauveine, revolutionised the world of fashion and made him rich. He opened a highly successful factory in North Greenford by the canal.

In 2023, a family of five Eurasian Beavers were released in the reedbeds and lagoons of **Paradise Fields**, 400 years after they were hunted to extinction in England, as part of a project to create a thriving wetland environment.

Greenford's origins are Saxon, the name *Grenan forda*, referring to the 'green ford' across the River Brent. It remained no more than a village until its rail and road connections and surfeit of open land attracted companies to set up factories in the 1920s, including Lyons Tea, Glaxo Laboratories and Rockware Glass, remembered in the name of Rockware Avenue.

The A40 initially ran through open fields, but, by the late 1930s, most of the green spaces had been lost under streets and houses. **Cayton Green Park** was preserved as playing fields and is now home to Northolt Rugby Football Club and Tara Gaelic Football Club, one of the biggest Gaelic football clubs in London.

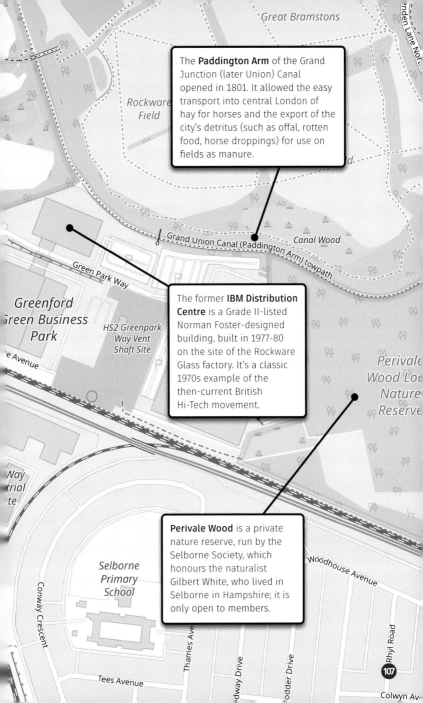

The **Paddington Arm** of the Grand Junction (later Union) Canal opened in 1801. It allowed the easy transport into central London of hay for horses and the export of the city's detritus (such as offal, rotten food, horse droppings) for use on fields as manure.

The former **IBM Distribution Centre** is a Grade II-listed Norman Foster-designed building, built in 1977-80 on the site of the Rockware Glass factory. It's a classic 1970s example of the then-current British Hi-Tech movement.

Perivale Wood is a private nature reserve, run by the Selborne Society, which honours the naturalist Gilbert White, who lived in Selborne in Hampshire; it is only open to members.

Great Bramstons

Rockware Field

Grand Union Canal (Paddington Arm) towpath

Canal Wood

Green Park Way

Greenford Green Business Park

HS2 Greenpark Way Vent Shaft Site

Perivale Wood Local Nature Reserve

Selborne Primary School

Conway Crescent

Woodhouse Avenue

Rhyl Road

Thames Ave

Tees Avenue

Colwyn Av

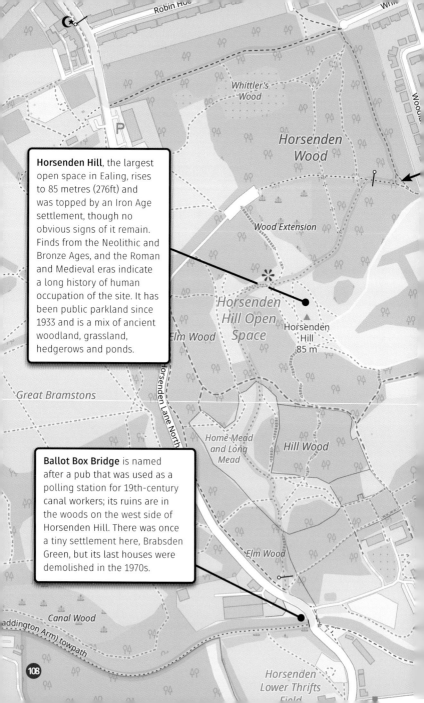

Horsenden Hill, the largest open space in Ealing, rises to 85 metres (276ft) and was topped by an Iron Age settlement, though no obvious signs of it remain. Finds from the Neolithic and Bronze Ages, and the Roman and Medieval eras indicate a long history of human occupation of the site. It has been public parkland since 1933 and is a mix of ancient woodland, grassland, hedgerows and ponds.

Ballot Box Bridge is named after a pub that was used as a polling station for 19th-century canal workers; its ruins are in the woods on the west side of Horsenden Hill. There was once a tiny settlement here, Brabsden Green, but its last houses were demolished in the 1970s.

Robin Hood

Whittler's Wood

Horsenden Wood

Wood Extension

Horsenden Hill Open Space

Elm Wood

Horsenden Hill 85 m

Great Bramstons

Horsenden Lane North

Home Mead and Long Mead

Hill Wood

Elm Wood

Canal Wood

addington Arm) towpath

Horsenden Lower Thrifts Field

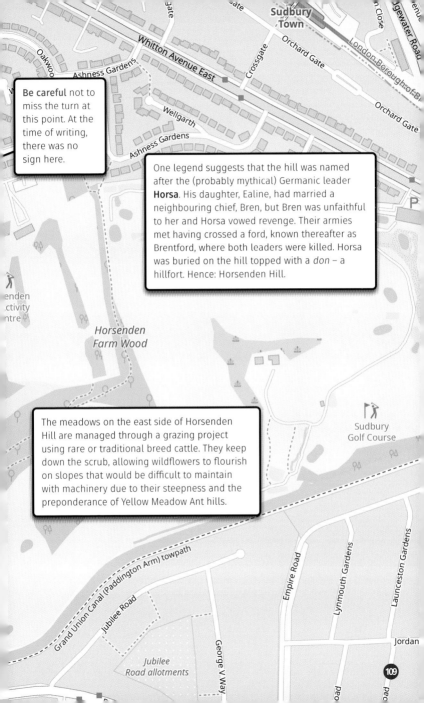

Be careful not to miss the turn at this point. At the time of writing, there was no sign here.

One legend suggests that the hill was named after the (probably mythical) Germanic leader **Horsa**. His daughter, Ealine, had married a neighbouring chief, Bren, but Bren was unfaithful to her and Horsa vowed revenge. Their armies met having crossed a ford, known thereafter as Brentford, where both leaders were killed. Horsa was buried on the hill topped with a *don* – a hillfort. Hence: Horsenden Hill.

The meadows on the east side of Horsenden Hill are managed through a grazing project using rare or traditional breed cattle. They keep down the scrub, allowing wildflowers to flourish on slopes that would be difficult to maintain with machinery due to their steepness and the preponderance of Yellow Meadow Ant hills.

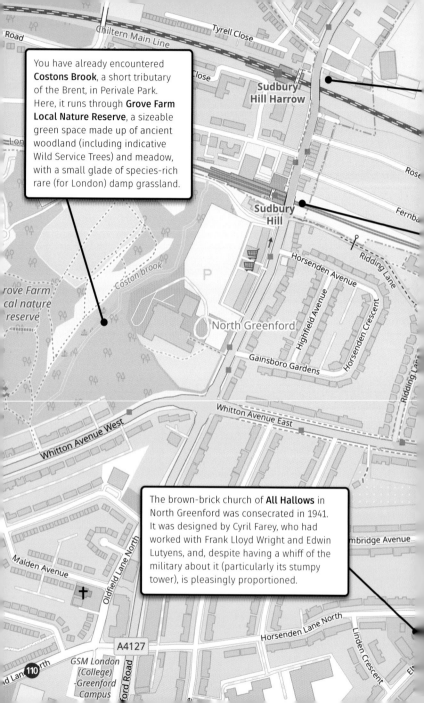

You have already encountered **Costons Brook**, a short tributary of the Brent, in Perivale Park. Here, it runs through **Grove Farm Local Nature Reserve**, a sizeable green space made up of ancient woodland (including indicative Wild Service Trees) and meadow, with a small glade of species-rich rare (for London) damp grassland.

The brown-brick church of **All Hallows** in North Greenford was consecrated in 1941. It was designed by Cyril Farey, who had worked with Frank Lloyd Wright and Edwin Lutyens, and, despite having a whiff of the military about it (particularly its stumpy tower), is pleasingly proportioned.

Road

Chiltern Main Line

Tyrell Close

Close

Sudbury Hill Harrow

Rose

Lon

Fernba

Sudbury Hill

Ridding Lane

Horsenden Avenue

Rose

P

Highfield Avenue

Horsenden Crescent

rove Farm cal nature reserve

Coston brook

North Greenford

Ridding Lane

Gainsboro Gardens

Whitton Avenue East

Whitton Avenue West

mbridge Avenue

Malden Avenue

Oldfield Lane North

Horsenden Lane North

Linden Crescent

A4127

GSM London (College) -Greenford Campus

110

rd Lan rth

ford Road

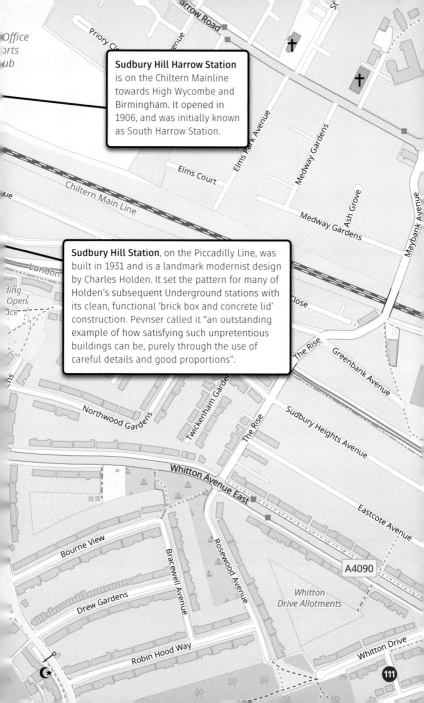

Sudbury Hill Harrow Station
is on the Chiltern Mainline towards High Wycombe and Birmingham. It opened in 1906, and was initially known as South Harrow Station.

Sudbury Hill Station, on the Piccadilly Line, was built in 1931 and is a landmark modernist design by Charles Holden. It set the pattern for many of Holden's subsequent Underground stations with its clean, functional 'brick box and concrete lid' construction. Pevsner called it "an outstanding example of how satisfying such unpretentious buildings can be, purely through the use of careful details and good proportions".

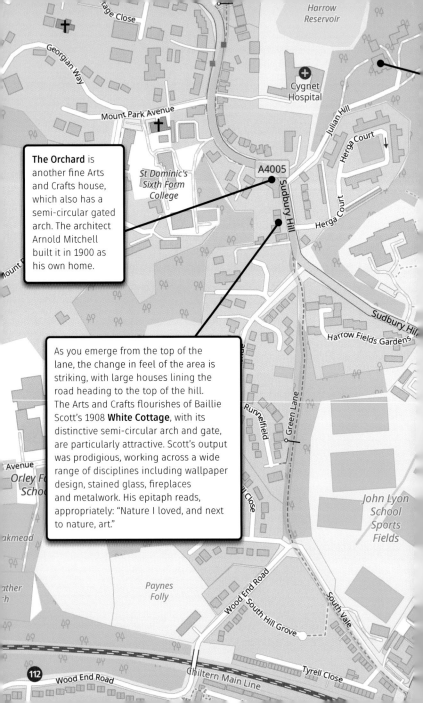

The Orchard is another fine Arts and Crafts house, which also has a semi-circular gated arch. The architect Arnold Mitchell built it in 1900 as his own home.

As you emerge from the top of the lane, the change in feel of the area is striking, with large houses lining the road heading to the top of the hill. The Arts and Crafts flourishes of Baillie Scott's 1908 **White Cottage**, with its distinctive semi-circular arch and gate, are particularly attractive. Scott's output was prodigious, working across a wide range of disciplines including wallpaper design, stained glass, fireplaces and metalwork. His epitaph reads, appropriately: "Nature I loved, and next to nature, art."

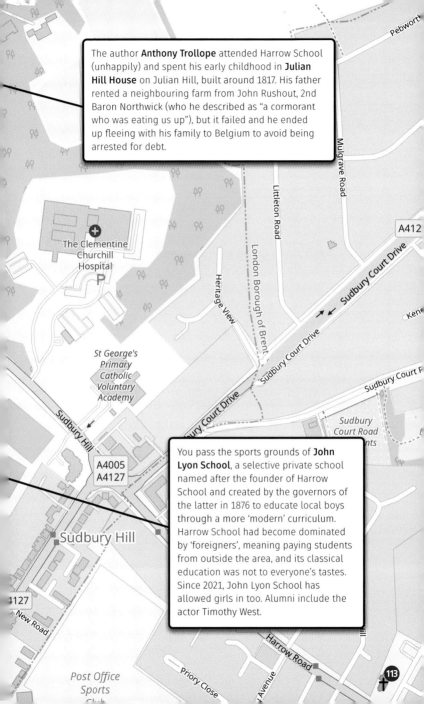

The author **Anthony Trollope** attended Harrow School (unhappily) and spent his early childhood in **Julian Hill House** on Julian Hill, built around 1817. His father rented a neighbouring farm from John Rushout, 2nd Baron Northwick (who he described as "a cormorant who was eating us up"), but it failed and he ended up fleeing with his family to Belgium to avoid being arrested for debt.

You pass the sports grounds of **John Lyon School**, a selective private school named after the founder of Harrow School and created by the governors of the latter in 1876 to educate local boys through a more 'modern' curriculum. Harrow School had become dominated by 'foreigners', meaning paying students from outside the area, and its classical education was not to everyone's tastes. Since 2021, John Lyon School has allowed girls in too. Alumni include the actor Timothy West.

Pebwort

Mulgrave Road

Littleton Road

London Borough of Brent

A412

Sudbury Court Drive

Ken

Heritage View

The Clementine Churchill Hospital

St George's Primary Catholic Voluntary Academy

Sudbury Hill

Sudbury Court Drive

Sudbury Court Drive

Sudbury Court F

Sudbury Court Road
nts

A4005
A4127

Sudbury Hill

1127

New Road

Post Office Sports
Club

Harrow Road

Priory Close

Avenue

113

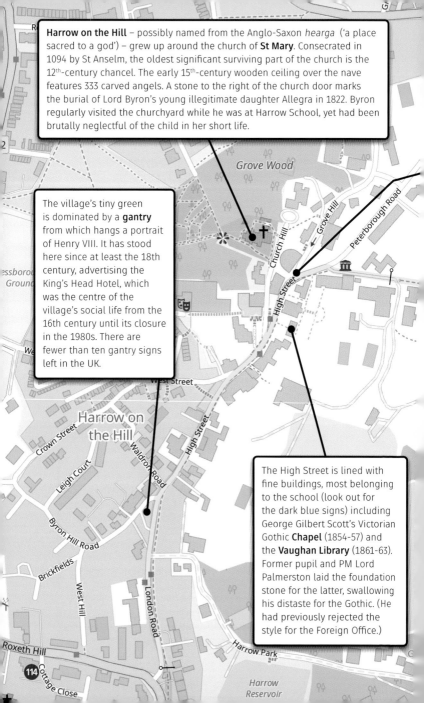

Harrow on the Hill – possibly named from the Anglo-Saxon *hearga* ('a place sacred to a god') – grew up around the church of **St Mary**. Consecrated in 1094 by St Anselm, the oldest significant surviving part of the church is the 12th-century chancel. The early 15th-century wooden ceiling over the nave features 333 carved angels. A stone to the right of the church door marks the burial of Lord Byron's young illegitimate daughter Allegra in 1822. Byron regularly visited the churchyard while he was at Harrow School, yet had been brutally neglectful of the child in her short life.

The village's tiny green is dominated by a **gantry** from which hangs a portrait of Henry VIII. It has stood here since at least the 18th century, advertising the King's Head Hotel, which was the centre of the village's social life from the 16th century until its closure in the 1980s. There are fewer than ten gantry signs left in the UK.

The High Street is lined with fine buildings, most belonging to the school (look out for the dark blue signs) including George Gilbert Scott's Victorian Gothic **Chapel** (1854-57) and the **Vaughan Library** (1861-63). Former pupil and PM Lord Palmerston laid the foundation stone for the latter, swallowing his distaste for the Gothic. (He had previously rejected the style for the Foreign Office.)

A **plaque** warns 'Take Heed'. Grove Hill saw the UK's first petrol-powered **motoring fatality** causing the death of a driver when, on 25th February 1899, a rear wheel of Edwin Sewell's Daimler collapsed as he sped down the hill at 20mph. Both he and his passenger were thrown from the car and died.

The village is dominated by its famous public school. **Harrow School** was founded in 1572 by John Lyon, a wealthy local farmer, to provide free education to poor local boys. It is now a boarding school with fees in excess of £16,000 per term, and an alumni list that includes Lord Byron, Jawaharlal Nehru and seven British PMs, including Winston Churchill.

Harrow Hill Golf Course

thwick Walk

pper Fi

Ducker Fields

ds Lane

ane

Julian 1

Julian 2

Sunley Field

Harrow School

ord Road

Ducker Fi

Watford Road

Harrow's most celebrated former pupil is undoubtedly **Winston Churchill**. He arrived in 1888 aged 13, shooed in by the sympathetic Headmaster, despite performing poorly on the entrance exam. Despite his great love for history and poetry, Churchill always struggled with Latin, and was mocked for it by his fellow pupils. As he later wrote, "I was on the whole considerably discouraged by my school days."

Controversy has not been a stranger to Harrow School in recent years. In 2005, it was one of 50 top independent schools found guilty of illegal price-fixing, and for much of the last 20 years disputes have rumbled on about access to footpaths across the sports pitches beneath the school, including the Capital Ring. Walkers and locals have usually emerged triumphant. You do have the right to walk diagonally across the rugby pitches here if you wish.

London Borough of Ha

rth Road

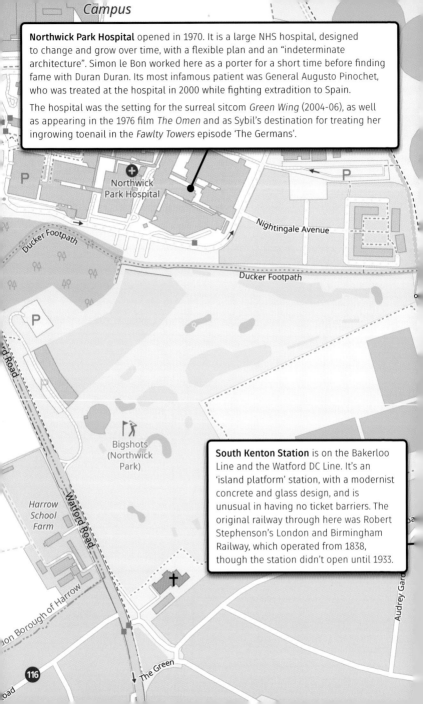

Northwick Park Hospital opened in 1970. It is a large NHS hospital, designed to change and grow over time, with a flexible plan and an "indeterminate architecture". Simon le Bon worked here as a porter for a short time before finding fame with Duran Duran. Its most infamous patient was General Augusto Pinochet, who was treated at the hospital in 2000 while fighting extradition to Spain.

The hospital was the setting for the surreal sitcom *Green Wing* (2004-06), as well as appearing in the 1976 film *The Omen* and as Sybil's destination for treating her ingrowing toenail in the *Fawlty Towers* episode 'The Germans'.

Northwick
Park Hospital

Nightingale Avenue

Ducker Footpath

Ducker Footpath

Bigshots
(Northwick
Park)

Harrow
School
Farm

Watford Road

South Kenton Station is on the Bakerloo Line and the Watford DC Line. It's an 'island platform' station, with a modernist concrete and glass design, and is unusual in having no ticket barriers. The original railway through here was Robert Stephenson's London and Birmingham Railway, which operated from 1838, though the station didn't open until 1933.

on Borough of Harrow

The Green

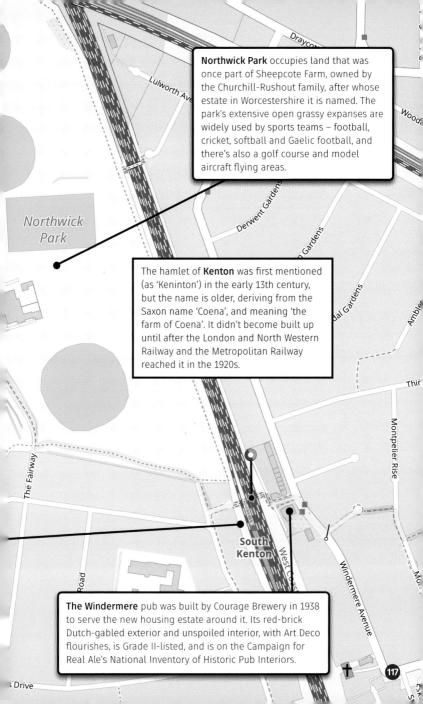

Northwick Park occupies land that was once part of Sheepcote Farm, owned by the Churchill-Rushout family, after whose estate in Worcestershire it is named. The park's extensive open grassy expanses are widely used by sports teams – football, cricket, softball and Gaelic football, and there's also a golf course and model aircraft flying areas.

The hamlet of **Kenton** was first mentioned (as 'Keninton') in the early 13th century, but the name is older, deriving from the Saxon name 'Coena', and meaning 'the farm of Coena'. It didn't become built up until after the London and North Western Railway and the Metropolitan Railway reached it in the 1920s.

The Windermere pub was built by Courage Brewery in 1938 to serve the new housing estate around it. Its red-brick Dutch-gabled exterior and unspoiled interior, with Art Deco flourishes, is Grade II-listed, and is on the Campaign for Real Ale's National Inventory of Historic Pub Interiors.

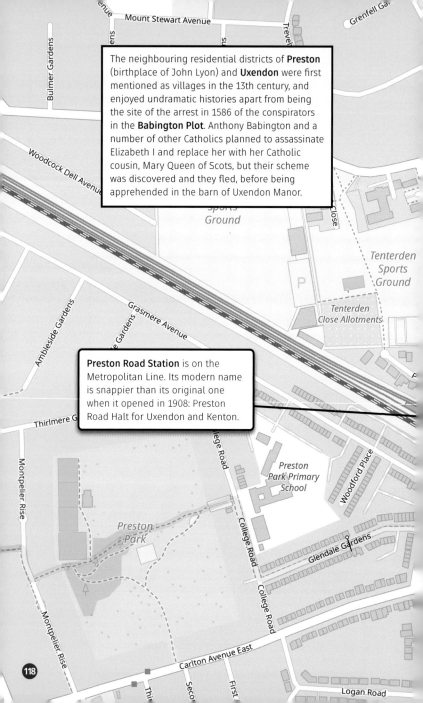

The neighbouring residential districts of **Preston** (birthplace of John Lyon) and **Uxendon** were first mentioned as villages in the 13th century, and enjoyed undramatic histories apart from being the site of the arrest in 1586 of the conspirators in the **Babington Plot**. Anthony Babington and a number of other Catholics planned to assassinate Elizabeth I and replace her with her Catholic cousin, Mary Queen of Scots, but their scheme was discovered and they fled, before being apprehended in the barn of Uxendon Manor.

Preston Road Station is on the Metropolitan Line. Its modern name is snappier than its original one when it opened in 1908: Preston Road Halt for Uxendon and Kenton.

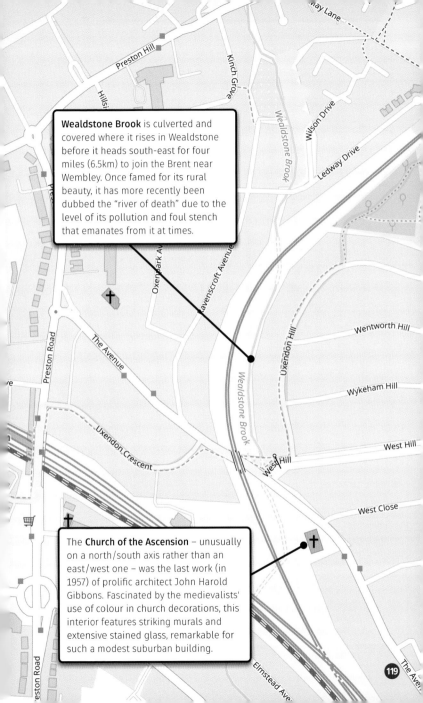

Wealdstone Brook is culverted and covered where it rises in Wealdstone before it heads south-east for four miles (6.5km) to join the Brent near Wembley. Once famed for its rural beauty, it has more recently been dubbed the "river of death" due to the level of its pollution and foul stench that emanates from it at times.

The **Church of the Ascension** – unusually on a north/south axis rather than an east/west one – was the last work (in 1957) of prolific architect John Harold Gibbons. Fascinated by the medievalists' use of colour in church decorations, this interior features striking murals and extensive stained glass, remarkable for such a modest suburban building.

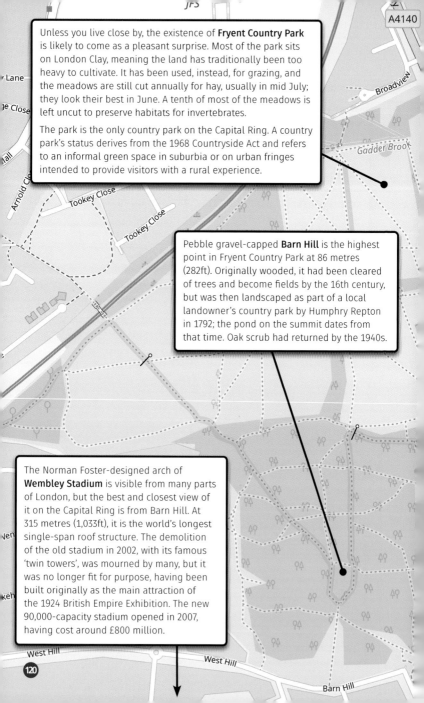

Unless you live close by, the existence of **Fryent Country Park** is likely to come as a pleasant surprise. Most of the park sits on London Clay, meaning the land has traditionally been too heavy to cultivate. It has been used, instead, for grazing, and the meadows are still cut annually for hay, usually in mid July; they look their best in June. A tenth of most of the meadows is left uncut to preserve habitats for invertebrates.

The park is the only country park on the Capital Ring. A country park's status derives from the 1968 Countryside Act and refers to an informal green space in suburbia or on urban fringes intended to provide visitors with a rural experience.

Pebble gravel-capped **Barn Hill** is the highest point in Fryent Country Park at 86 metres (282ft). Originally wooded, it had been cleared of trees and become fields by the 16th century, but was then landscaped as part of a local landowner's country park by Humphry Repton in 1792; the pond on the summit dates from that time. Oak scrub had returned by the 1940s.

The Norman Foster-designed arch of **Wembley Stadium** is visible from many parts of London, but the best and closest view of it on the Capital Ring is from Barn Hill. At 315 metres (1,033ft), it is the world's longest single-span roof structure. The demolition of the old stadium in 2002, with its famous 'twin towers', was mourned by many, but it was no longer fit for purpose, having been built originally as the main attraction of the 1924 British Empire Exhibition. The new 90,000-capacity stadium opened in 2007, having cost around £800 million.

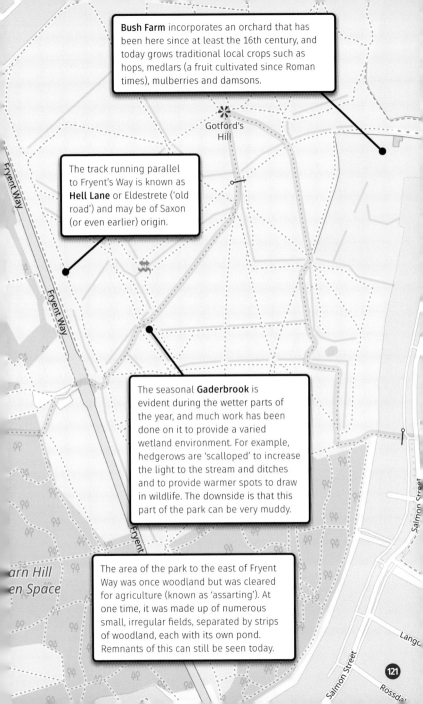

Bush Farm incorporates an orchard that has been here since at least the 16th century, and today grows traditional local crops such as hops, medlars (a fruit cultivated since Roman times), mulberries and damsons.

Gotford's Hill

The track running parallel to Fryent's Way is known as **Hell Lane** or Eldestrete ('old road') and may be of Saxon (or even earlier) origin.

Fryent Way

The seasonal **Gaderbrook** is evident during the wetter parts of the year, and much work has been done on it to provide a varied wetland environment. For example, hedgerows are 'scalloped' to increase the light to the stream and ditches and to provide warmer spots to draw in wildlife. The downside is that this part of the park can be very muddy.

arn Hill
en Space

The area of the park to the east of Fryent Way was once woodland but was cleared for agriculture (known as 'assarting'). At one time, it was made up of numerous small, irregular fields, separated by strips of woodland, each with its own pond. Remnants of this can still be seen today.

Salmon Street

Langc

Salmon Street

Rossda'

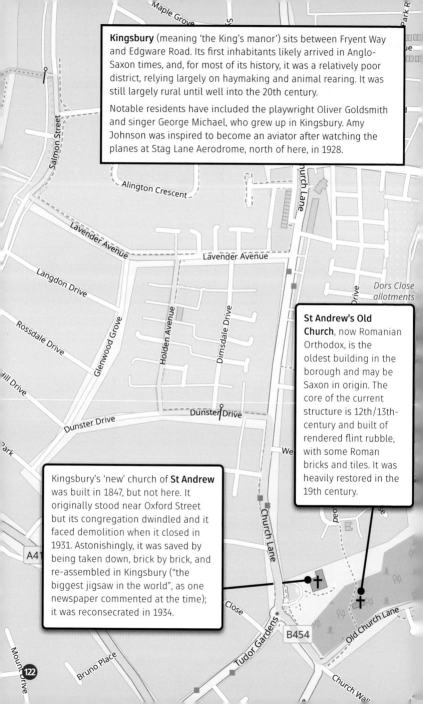

Kingsbury (meaning 'the King's manor') sits between Fryent Way and Edgware Road. Its first inhabitants likely arrived in Anglo-Saxon times, and, for most of its history, it was a relatively poor district, relying largely on haymaking and animal rearing. It was still largely rural until well into the 20th century.

Notable residents have included the playwright Oliver Goldsmith and singer George Michael, who grew up in Kingsbury. Amy Johnson was inspired to become an aviator after watching the planes at Stag Lane Aerodrome, north of here, in 1928.

St Andrew's Old Church, now Romanian Orthodox, is the oldest building in the borough and may be Saxon in origin. The core of the current structure is 12th/13th-century and built of rendered flint rubble, with some Roman bricks and tiles. It was heavily restored in the 19th century.

Kingsbury's 'new' church of **St Andrew** was built in 1847, but not here. It originally stood near Oxford Street but its congregation dwindled and it faced demolition when it closed in 1931. Astonishingly, it was saved by being taken down, brick by brick, and re-assembled in Kingsbury ("the biggest jigsaw in the world", as one newspaper commented at the time); it was reconsecrated in 1934.

During the 1920s, **naturists** enjoyed sunning themselves at a secluded spot by the reservoir, but, in the summer of 1930, objectors whipped themselves up into a frenzy of prurient self-righteousness, attacking the sunbathers, and the local council was eventually embarrassed into banning the practice. Evelyn Waugh wrote: "The people who made such a fuss at the Welsh Harp simply detest the spectacle of bodies of any kind, beautiful or ugly... These astonishing people assemble in a large crowd at the one place where they know they will see the very thing which displeases them."

Since the reservoir was built, it has attracted large numbers of **birds**, many of which were uncommon. Early ornithologists showed their enthusiasm by shooting and stuffing many of them, but it remains a noted spot for twitchers today. More than 250 species have been recorded here, and it is an important breeding site for many birds, such as the Great Crested Grebe. Invertebrates also thrive at Welsh Harp, drawing in notable numbers of bats of many different species, including the tiny Nathusius' Pipistrelle.

Brent Reservoir, more popularly known as the **Welsh Harp**, was created in the 1830s when the River Brent was dammed at Kingsbury to provide water for London's canals. The reservoir has been reduced in size over the years and is now only a quarter of its original extent. Littering has been a major issue in the reservoir, but it was drained and cleaned up in early 2024.

Kingsbury local **William Perkins Warner** became the landlord of the **Old Welsh Harp** by the Edgware Road in 1858, next to the (then much larger) reservoir. A horse-drawn bus service between London and Edgware had just started, and Warner provided attractions to draw in passengers – with spectacular success. For 40 years, it was one of the most popular day-trip destinations from London. The pub was demolished in 1971 to make way for Staples Corner at the start of the M1.

William Warner's vision was a grand one. He rebuilt the tavern, with a huge dining room for music hall entertainment, pleasure gardens, sports facilities, and with fishing and boating on the water, and ice skating in winter. Boxing matches, swimming galas and horse races drew in big crowds. Britain's first formal bicycle race took place in a meadow by the reservoir in 1868.

The listed **Cool Oak Lane Bridge** was created in the 1830s to cross the two arms of the reservoir.

Warner had a gift for publicity. Around 1864, he had new words written for a popular music hall song by Annie Adams, who performed it at the pub.

'Warner's Welsh Harp! – Have you ever been there?
Pic-nics, with tricks: ev'ry day are seen there,
You couldn't find its equal, if you walked for miles about,
There's no mistake about it – it's the Jolliest Place That's Out.

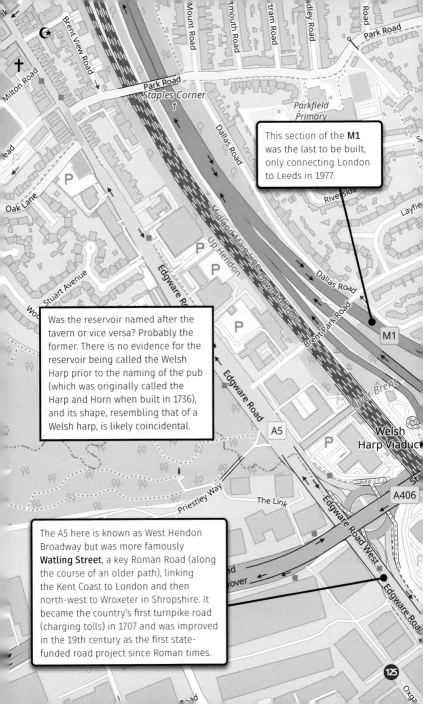

This section of the **M1** was the last to be built, only connecting London to Leeds in 1977.

Was the reservoir named after the tavern or vice versa? Probably the former. There is no evidence for the reservoir being called the Welsh Harp prior to the naming of the pub (which was originally called the Harp and Horn when built in 1736), and its shape, resembling that of a Welsh harp, is likely coincidental.

The A5 here is known as West Hendon Broadway but was more famously **Watling Street**, a key Roman Road (along the course of an older path), linking the Kent Coast to London and then north-west to Wroxeter in Shropshire. It became the country's first turnpike road (charging tolls) in 1707 and was improved in the 19th century as the first state-funded road project since Roman times.

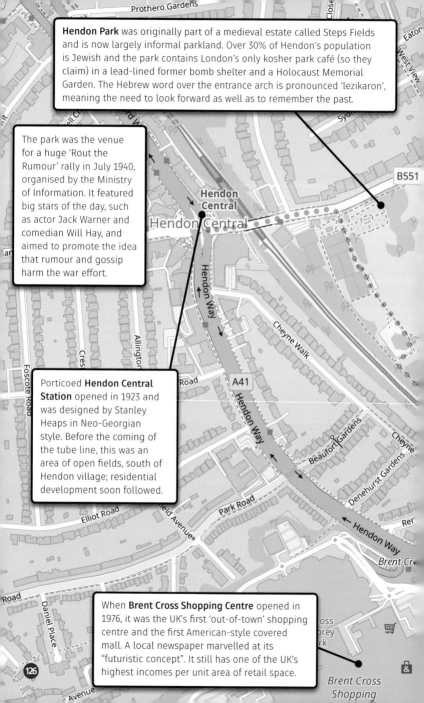

Hendon Park was originally part of a medieval estate called Steps Fields and is now largely informal parkland. Over 30% of Hendon's population is Jewish and the park contains London's only kosher park café (so they claim) in a lead-lined former bomb shelter and a Holocaust Memorial Garden. The Hebrew word over the entrance arch is pronounced 'lezikaron', meaning the need to look forward as well as to remember the past.

The park was the venue for a huge 'Rout the Rumour' rally in July 1940, organised by the Ministry of Information. It featured big stars of the day, such as actor Jack Warner and comedian Will Hay, and aimed to promote the idea that rumour and gossip harm the war effort.

Porticoed **Hendon Central Station** opened in 1923 and was designed by Stanley Heaps in Neo-Georgian style. Before the coming of the tube line, this was an area of open fields, south of Hendon village; residential development soon followed.

When **Brent Cross Shopping Centre** opened in 1976, it was the UK's first 'out-of-town' shopping centre and the first American-style covered mall. A local newspaper marvelled at its "futuristic concept". It still has one of the UK's highest incomes per unit area of retail space.

Brent Bridge House, an 18th-century mansion and, later, a hotel, stood on this site until it was demolished in the 1970s. It takes a leap of imagination to picture it as the lush and tranquil spot it once was, favoured by gentlemen to relax and convalesce. All that remains are the dilapidated, graffiti-sprayed brick summerhouses on either side of the river.

Hendon, meaning 'at the highest hill', was settled by the time of the Domesday Book, but people have lived in this area since Roman times. Its southern reaches are dominated by transport links – the North Circular Road, the M1, Edgware Road and mainline and underground train lines.

Several local roads carry the name **Shirehall**, referring to an 18th-century country house that stood nearby in what was then largely undeveloped countryside. Penfold House, on the corner of Shirehall Lane and Brent Street, dates from 1713 and was once a hostel for drovers.

You may wish to briefly detour to admire Emile Guillaume's statue *La Delivrance*, known locally as **'The Naked Lady'**. It was created to celebrate the halting of the German advance at the 1st Battle of the Marne in September 1914. The original was admired by Viscount Rothermere, proprietor of the *Daily Mail*, who had this copy commissioned.

Dollis Brook, rising in Mill Hill, becomes the River Brent at the spot where it meets Mutton Brook. Its name may come from the Middle English word 'dole', which means a share in a common field.

The pond known as **The Decoy** may be part of a 1000-year-old lake created for the Abbots of Westminster as a duck decoy. This was a type of small lake with narrow channels running into it. Nets were set at the ends of the channels and waterfowl chased into them by dogs. It is possible the name is derived from the Dutch *eendenkooi*, meaning 'duck cage'; few remain in the UK, though they are still relatively common in the Netherlands. Coots, Moorhens, Mallards and Tufted Ducks still nest on the island in the pond.

The narrow, heavily wooded strip of **Brent Park** is hemmed in by the river and the North Circular but provides a valuable green corridor. It was once part of Decoy Wood in the grounds of the now demolished Brent Bridge House and opened as a public park in 1934.

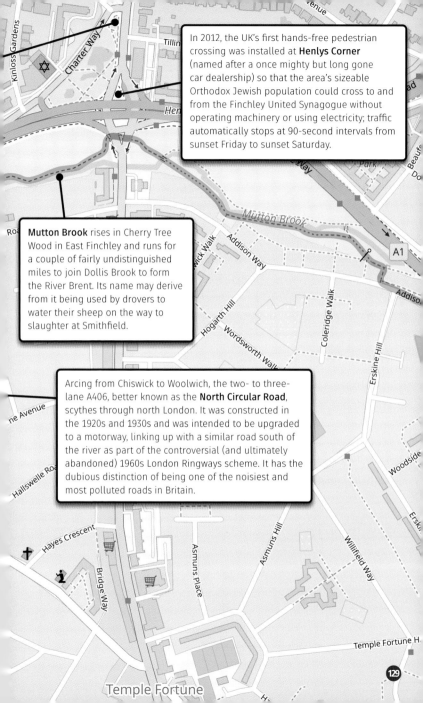

In 2012, the UK's first hands-free pedestrian crossing was installed at **Henlys Corner** (named after a once mighty but long gone car dealership) so that the area's sizeable Orthodox Jewish population could cross to and from the Finchley United Synagogue without operating machinery or using electricity; traffic automatically stops at 90-second intervals from sunset Friday to sunset Saturday.

Mutton Brook rises in Cherry Tree Wood in East Finchley and runs for a couple of fairly undistinguished miles to join Dollis Brook to form the River Brent. Its name may derive from it being used by drovers to water their sheep on the way to slaughter at Smithfield.

Arcing from Chiswick to Woolwich, the two- to three-lane A406, better known as the **North Circular Road**, scythes through north London. It was constructed in the 1920s and 1930s and was intended to be upgraded to a motorway, linking up with a similar road south of the river as part of the controversial (and ultimately abandoned) 1960s London Ringways scheme. It has the dubious distinction of being one of the noisiest and most polluted roads in Britain.

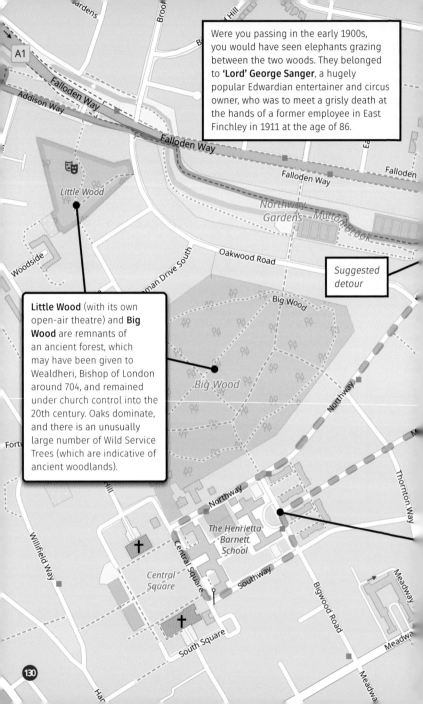

Were you passing in the early 1900s, you would have seen elephants grazing between the two woods. They belonged to **'Lord' George Sanger**, a hugely popular Edwardian entertainer and circus owner, who was to meet a grisly death at the hands of a former employee in East Finchley in 1911 at the age of 86.

Suggested detour

Little Wood (with its own open-air theatre) and **Big Wood** are remnants of an ancient forest, which may have been given to Wealdheri, Bishop of London around 704, and remained under church control into the 20th century. Oaks dominate, and there is an unusually large number of Wild Service Trees (which are indicative of ancient woodlands).

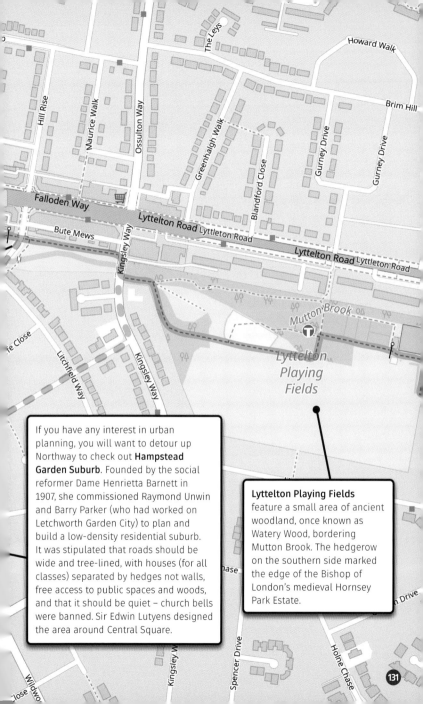

If you have any interest in urban planning, you will want to detour up Northway to check out **Hampstead Garden Suburb**. Founded by the social reformer Dame Henrietta Barnett in 1907, she commissioned Raymond Unwin and Barry Parker (who had worked on Letchworth Garden City) to plan and build a low-density residential suburb. It was stipulated that roads should be wide and tree-lined, with houses (for all classes) separated by hedges not walls, free access to public spaces and woods, and that it should be quiet – church bells were banned. Sir Edwin Lutyens designed the area around Central Square.

Lyttelton Playing Fields
feature a small area of ancient woodland, once known as Watery Wood, bordering Mutton Brook. The hedgerow on the southern side marked the edge of the Bishop of London's medieval Hornsey Park Estate.

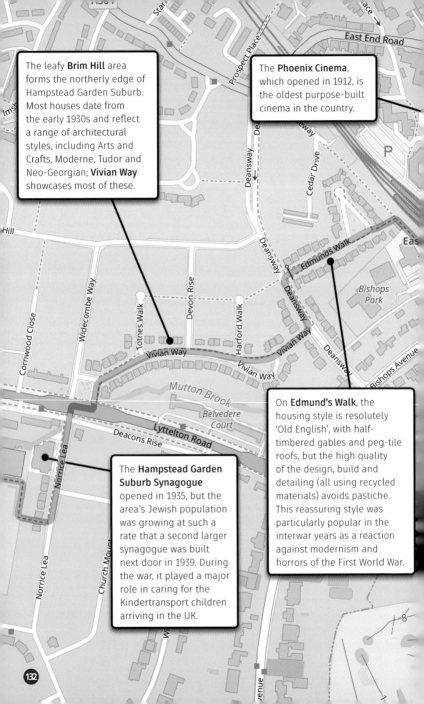

The leafy **Brim Hill** area forms the northerly edge of Hampstead Garden Suburb. Most houses date from the early 1930s and reflect a range of architectural styles, including Arts and Crafts, Moderne, Tudor and Neo-Georgian; **Vivian Way** showcases most of these.

The **Phoenix Cinema**, which opened in 1912, is the oldest purpose-built cinema in the country.

On **Edmund's Walk**, the housing style is resolutely 'Old English', with half-timbered gables and peg-tile roofs, but the high quality of the design, build and detailing (all using recycled materials) avoids pastiche. This reassuring style was particularly popular in the interwar years as a reaction against modernism and horrors of the First World War.

The **Hampstead Garden Suburb Synagogue** opened in 1935, but the area's Jewish population was growing at such a rate that a second larger synagogue was built next door in 1939. During the war, it played a major role in caring for the Kindertransport children arriving in the UK.

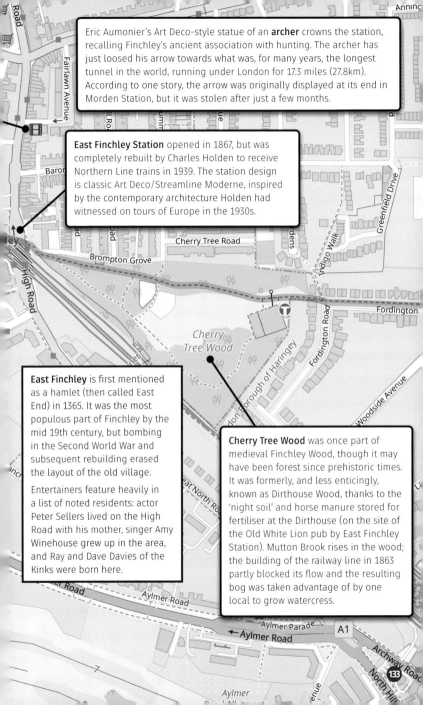

Eric Aumonier's Art Deco-style statue of an **archer** crowns the station, recalling Finchley's ancient association with hunting. The archer has just loosed his arrow towards what was, for many years, the longest tunnel in the world, running under London for 17.3 miles (27.8km). According to one story, the arrow was originally displayed at its end in Morden Station, but it was stolen after just a few months.

East Finchley Station opened in 1867, but was completely rebuilt by Charles Holden to receive Northern Line trains in 1939. The station design is classic Art Deco/Streamline Moderne, inspired by the contemporary architecture Holden had witnessed on tours of Europe in the 1930s.

East Finchley is first mentioned as a hamlet (then called East End) in 1365. It was the most populous part of Finchley by the mid 19th century, but bombing in the Second World War and subsequent rebuilding erased the layout of the old village.

Entertainers feature heavily in a list of noted residents: actor Peter Sellers lived on the High Road with his mother, singer Amy Winehouse grew up in the area, and Ray and Dave Davies of the Kinks were born here.

Cherry Tree Wood was once part of medieval Finchley Wood, though it may have been forest since prehistoric times. It was formerly, and less enticingly, known as Dirthouse Wood, thanks to the 'night soil' and horse manure stored for fertiliser at the Dirthouse (on the site of the Old White Lion pub by East Finchley Station). Mutton Brook rises in the wood; the building of the railway line in 1863 partly blocked its flow and the resulting bog was taken advantage of by one local to grow watercress.

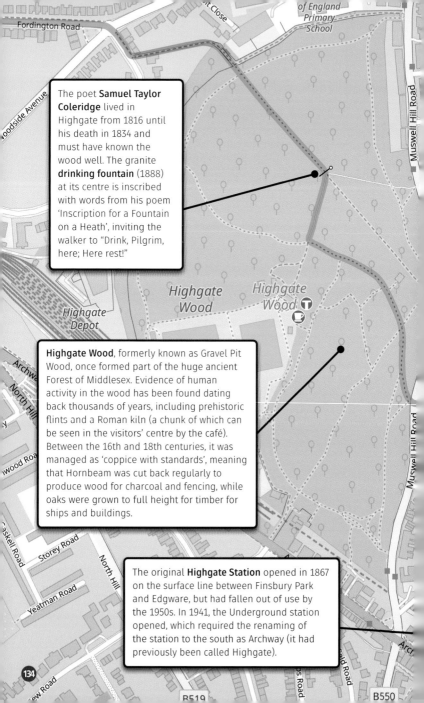

The poet **Samuel Taylor Coleridge** lived in Highgate from 1816 until his death in 1834 and must have known the wood well. The granite **drinking fountain** (1888) at its centre is inscribed with words from his poem 'Inscription for a Fountain on a Heath', inviting the walker to "Drink, Pilgrim, here; Here rest!"

Highgate Wood, formerly known as Gravel Pit Wood, once formed part of the huge ancient Forest of Middlesex. Evidence of human activity in the wood has been found dating back thousands of years, including prehistoric flints and a Roman kiln (a chunk of which can be seen in the visitors' centre by the café). Between the 16th and 18th centuries, it was managed as 'coppice with standards', meaning that Hornbeam was cut back regularly to produce wood for charcoal and fencing, while oaks were grown to full height for timber for ships and buildings.

The original **Highgate Station** opened in 1867 on the surface line between Finsbury Park and Edgware, but had fallen out of use by the 1950s. In 1941, the Underground station opened, which required the renaming of the station to the south as Archway (it had previously been called Highgate).

Fordington Road

Woodside Avenue

of England Primary School

Muswell Hill Road

Highgate Wood

Highgate Wood

Highgate Depot

Archw

North Hill

wood Roa

askell Road

Storey Road

North Hill

Yeatman Road

Muswell Hill Road

Arc

old Road

s Road

ew Road

B519

B550

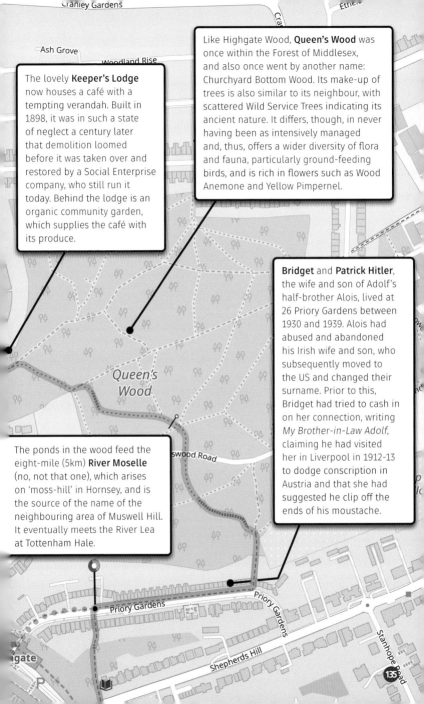

The lovely **Keeper's Lodge** now houses a café with a tempting verandah. Built in 1898, it was in such a state of neglect a century later that demolition loomed before it was taken over and restored by a Social Enterprise company, who still run it today. Behind the lodge is an organic community garden, which supplies the café with its produce.

Like Highgate Wood, **Queen's Wood** was once within the Forest of Middlesex, and also once went by another name: Churchyard Bottom Wood. Its make-up of trees is also similar to its neighbour, with scattered Wild Service Trees indicating its ancient nature. It differs, though, in never having been as intensively managed and, thus, offers a wider diversity of flora and fauna, particularly ground-feeding birds, and is rich in flowers such as Wood Anemone and Yellow Pimpernel.

Bridget and **Patrick Hitler**, the wife and son of Adolf's half-brother Alois, lived at 26 Priory Gardens between 1930 and 1939. Alois had abused and abandoned his Irish wife and son, who subsequently moved to the US and changed their surname. Prior to this, Bridget had tried to cash in on her connection, writing *My Brother-in-Law Adolf*, claiming he had visited her in Liverpool in 1912-13 to dodge conscription in Austria and that she had suggested he clip off the ends of his moustache.

The ponds in the wood feed the eight-mile (5km) **River Moselle** (no, not that one), which arises on 'moss-hill' in Hornsey, and is the source of the name of the neighbouring area of Muswell Hill. It eventually meets the River Lea at Tottenham Hale.

Queen's Wood

135

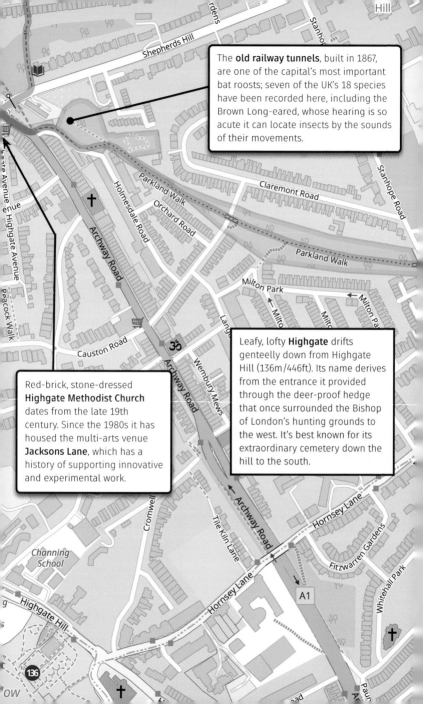

The **old railway tunnels**, built in 1867, are one of the capital's most important bat roosts; seven of the UK's 18 species have been recorded here, including the Brown Long-eared, whose hearing is so acute it can locate insects by the sounds of their movements.

Red-brick, stone-dressed **Highgate Methodist Church** dates from the late 19th century. Since the 1980s it has housed the multi-arts venue **Jacksons Lane**, which has a history of supporting innovative and experimental work.

Leafy, lofty **Highgate** drifts genteelly down from Highgate Hill (136m/446ft). Its name derives from the entrance it provided through the deer-proof hedge that once surrounded the Bishop of London's hunting grounds to the west. It's best known for its extraordinary cemetery down the hill to the south.

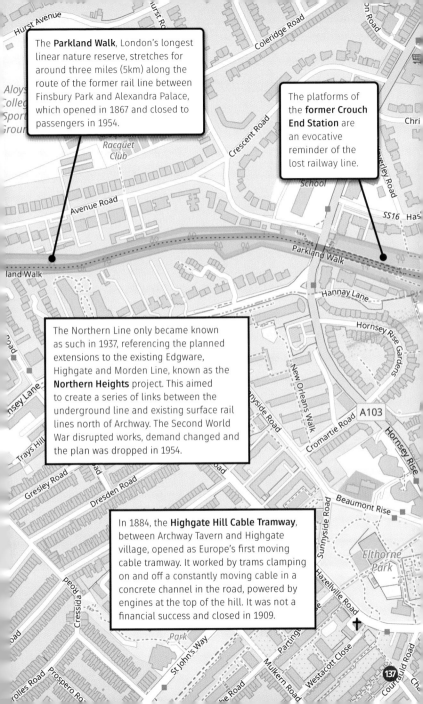

The **Parkland Walk**, London's longest linear nature reserve, stretches for around three miles (5km) along the route of the former rail line between Finsbury Park and Alexandra Palace, which opened in 1867 and closed to passengers in 1954.

The platforms of the **former Crouch End Station** are an evocative reminder of the lost railway line.

The Northern Line only became known as such in 1937, referencing the planned extensions to the existing Edgware, Highgate and Morden Line, known as the **Northern Heights** project. This aimed to create a series of links between the underground line and existing surface rail lines north of Archway. The Second World War disrupted works, demand changed and the plan was dropped in 1954.

In 1884, the **Highgate Hill Cable Tramway**, between Archway Tavern and Highgate village, opened as Europe's first moving cable tramway. It worked by trams clamping on and off a constantly moving cable in a concrete channel in the road, powered by engines at the top of the hill. It was not a financial success and closed in 1909.

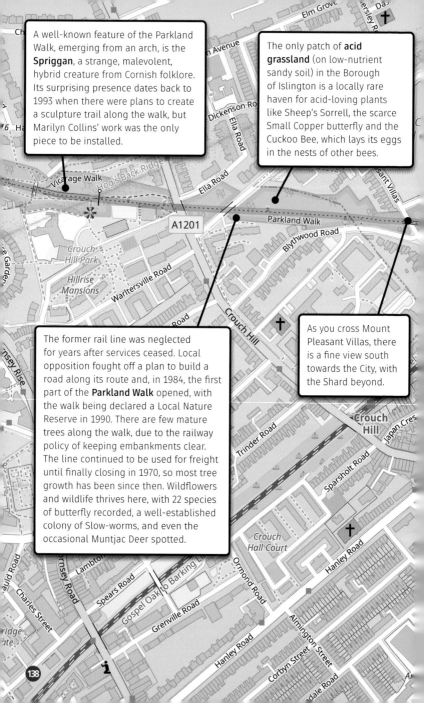

A well-known feature of the Parkland Walk, emerging from an arch, is the **Spriggan**, a strange, malevolent, hybrid creature from Cornish folklore. Its surprising presence dates back to 1993 when there were plans to create a sculpture trail along the walk, but Marilyn Collins' work was the only piece to be installed.

The only patch of **acid grassland** (on low-nutrient sandy soil) in the Borough of Islington is a locally rare haven for acid-loving plants like Sheep's Sorrell, the scarce Small Copper butterfly and the Cuckoo Bee, which lays its eggs in the nests of other bees.

The former rail line was neglected for years after services ceased. Local opposition fought off a plan to build a road along its route and, in 1984, the first part of the **Parkland Walk** opened, with the walk being declared a Local Nature Reserve in 1990. There are few mature trees along the walk, due to the railway policy of keeping embankments clear. The line continued to be used for freight until finally closing in 1970, so most tree growth has been since then. Wildflowers and wildlife thrives here, with 22 species of butterfly recorded, a well-established colony of Slow-worms, and even the occasional Muntjac Deer spotted.

As you cross Mount Pleasant Villas, there is a fine view south towards the City, with the Shard beyond.

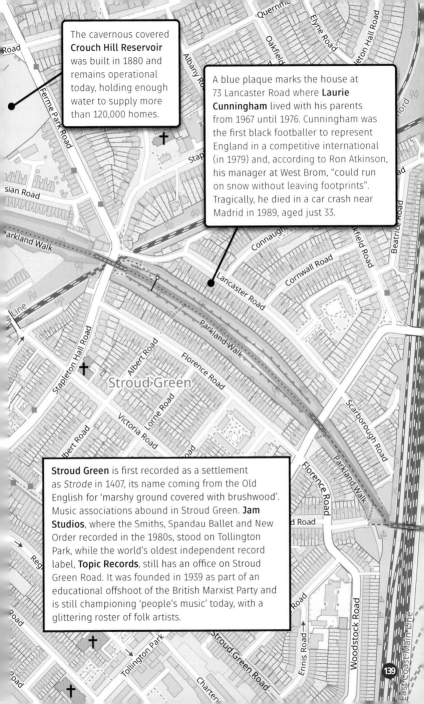

The cavernous covered **Crouch Hill Reservoir** was built in 1880 and remains operational today, holding enough water to supply more than 120,000 homes.

A blue plaque marks the house at 73 Lancaster Road where **Laurie Cunningham** lived with his parents from 1967 until 1976. Cunningham was the first black footballer to represent England in a competitive international (in 1979) and, according to Ron Atkinson, his manager at West Brom, "could run on snow without leaving footprints". Tragically, he died in a car crash near Madrid in 1989, aged just 33.

Stroud Green is first recorded as a settlement as *Strode* in 1407, its name coming from the Old English for 'marshy ground covered with brushwood'. Music associations abound in Stroud Green. **Jam Studios**, where the Smiths, Spandau Ballet and New Order recorded in the 1980s, stood on Tollington Park, while the world's oldest independent record label, **Topic Records**, still has an office on Stroud Green Road. It was founded in 1939 as part of an educational offshoot of the British Marxist Party and is still championing 'people's music' today, with a glittering roster of folk artists.

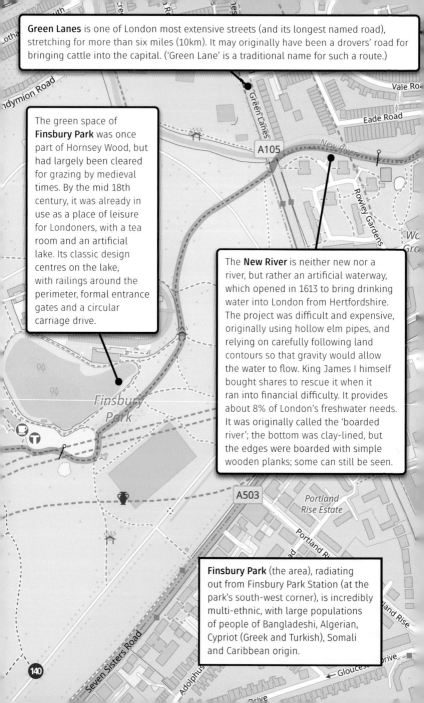

Green Lanes is one of London most extensive streets (and its longest named road), stretching more than six miles (10km). It may originally have been a drovers' road for bringing cattle into the capital. ('Green Lane' is a traditional name for such a route.)

The green space of **Finsbury Park** was once part of Hornsey Wood, but had largely been cleared for grazing by medieval times. By the mid 18th century, it was already in use as a place of leisure for Londoners, with a tea room and an artificial lake. Its classic design centres on the lake, with railings around the perimeter, formal entrance gates and a circular carriage drive.

The **New River** is neither new nor a river, but rather an artificial waterway, which opened in 1613 to bring drinking water into London from Hertfordshire. The project was difficult and expensive, originally using hollow elm pipes, and relying on carefully following land contours so that gravity would allow the water to flow. King James I himself bought shares to rescue it when it ran into financial difficulty. It provides about 8% of London's freshwater needs. It was originally called the 'boarded river'; the bottom was clay-lined, but the edges were boarded with simple wooden planks; some can still be seen.

Finsbury Park (the area), radiating out from Finsbury Park Station (at the park's south-west corner), is incredibly multi-ethnic, with large populations of people of Bangladeshi, Algerian, Cypriot (Greek and Turkish), Somali and Caribbean origin.

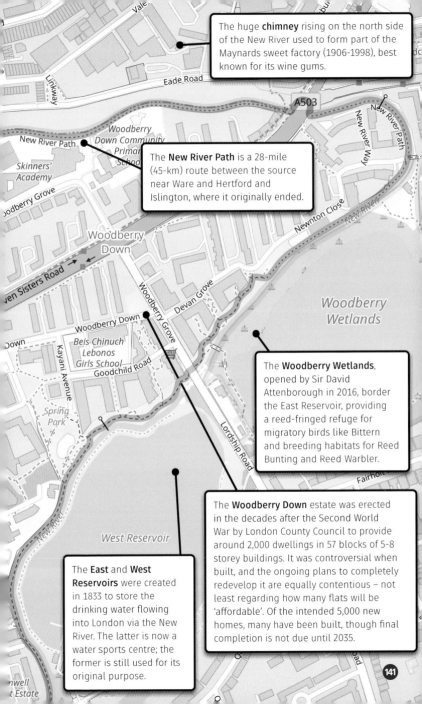

The huge **chimney** rising on the north side of the New River used to form part of the Maynards sweet factory (1906-1998), best known for its wine gums.

The **New River Path** is a 28-mile (45-km) route between the source near Ware and Hertford and Islington, where it originally ended.

The **Woodberry Wetlands**, opened by Sir David Attenborough in 2016, border the East Reservoir, providing a reed-fringed refuge for migratory birds like Bittern and breeding habitats for Reed Bunting and Reed Warbler.

The **Woodberry Down** estate was erected in the decades after the Second World War by London County Council to provide around 2,000 dwellings in 57 blocks of 5-8 storey buildings. It was controversial when built, and the ongoing plans to completely redevelop it are equally contentious – not least regarding how many flats will be 'affordable'. Of the intended 5,000 new homes, many have been built, though final completion is not due until 2035.

The **East** and **West Reservoirs** were created in 1833 to store the drinking water flowing into London via the New River. The latter is now a water sports centre; the former is still used for its original purpose.

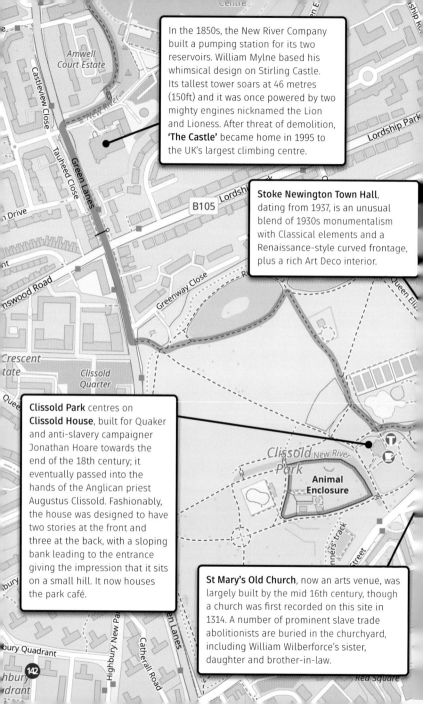

In the 1850s, the New River Company built a pumping station for its two reservoirs. William Mylne based his whimsical design on Stirling Castle. Its tallest tower soars at 46 metres (150ft) and it was once powered by two mighty engines nicknamed the Lion and Lioness. After threat of demolition, **'The Castle'** became home in 1995 to the UK's largest climbing centre.

Stoke Newington Town Hall, dating from 1937, is an unusual blend of 1930s monumentalism with Classical elements and a Renaissance-style curved frontage, plus a rich Art Deco interior.

Clissold Park centres on **Clissold House**, built for Quaker and anti-slavery campaigner Jonathan Hoare towards the end of the 18th century; it eventually passed into the hands of the Anglican priest Augustus Clissold. Fashionably, the house was designed to have two stories at the front and three at the back, with a sloping bank leading to the entrance giving the impression that it sits on a small hill. It now houses the park café.

St Mary's Old Church, now an arts venue, was largely built by the mid 16th century, though a church was first recorded on this site in 1314. A number of prominent slave trade abolitionists are buried in the churchyard, including William Wilberforce's sister, daughter and brother-in-law.

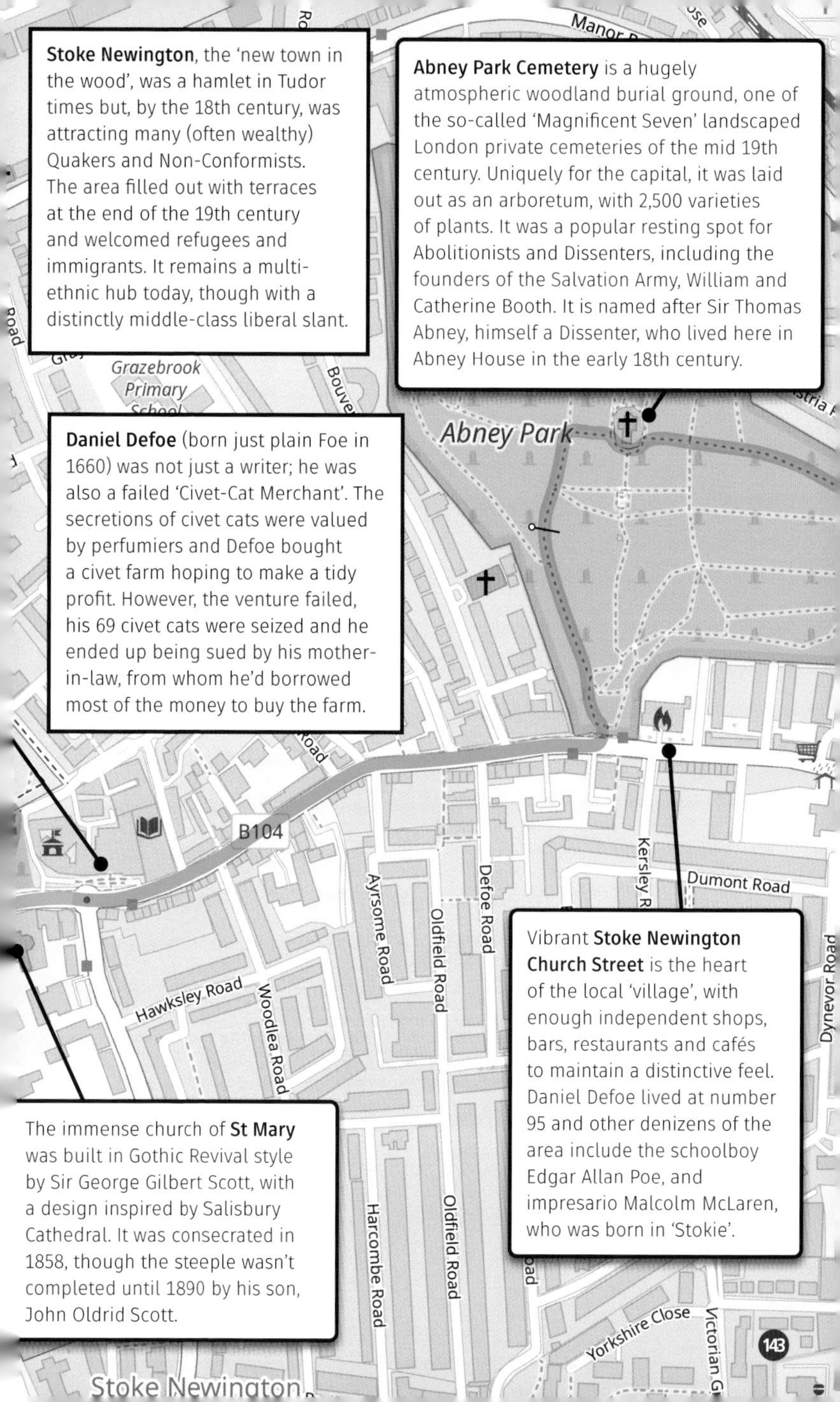

Stoke Newington, the 'new town in the wood', was a hamlet in Tudor times but, by the 18th century, was attracting many (often wealthy) Quakers and Non-Conformists. The area filled out with terraces at the end of the 19th century and welcomed refugees and immigrants. It remains a multi-ethnic hub today, though with a distinctly middle-class liberal slant.

Abney Park Cemetery is a hugely atmospheric woodland burial ground, one of the so-called 'Magnificent Seven' landscaped London private cemeteries of the mid 19th century. Uniquely for the capital, it was laid out as an arboretum, with 2,500 varieties of plants. It was a popular resting spot for Abolitionists and Dissenters, including the founders of the Salvation Army, William and Catherine Booth. It is named after Sir Thomas Abney, himself a Dissenter, who lived here in Abney House in the early 18th century.

Daniel Defoe (born just plain Foe in 1660) was not just a writer; he was also a failed 'Civet-Cat Merchant'. The secretions of civet cats were valued by perfumiers and Defoe bought a civet farm hoping to make a tidy profit. However, the venture failed, his 69 civet cats were seized and he ended up being sued by his mother-in-law, from whom he'd borrowed most of the money to buy the farm.

Vibrant **Stoke Newington Church Street** is the heart of the local 'village', with enough independent shops, bars, restaurants and cafés to maintain a distinctive feel. Daniel Defoe lived at number 95 and other denizens of the area include the schoolboy Edgar Allan Poe, and impresario Malcolm McLaren, who was born in 'Stokie'.

The immense church of **St Mary** was built in Gothic Revival style by Sir George Gilbert Scott, with a design inspired by Salisbury Cathedral. It was consecrated in 1858, though the steeple wasn't completed until 1890 by his son, John Oldrid Scott.

Map labels: Manor R..., ...use, Grazebrook Primary School, Abney Park, B104, Ayrsome Road, Oldfield Road, Defoe Road, Kersley R..., Dumont Road, Dynevor Road, Hawksley Road, Woodlea Road, Harcombe Road, Oldfield Road, Yorkshire Close, Victorian G..., Stoke Newington

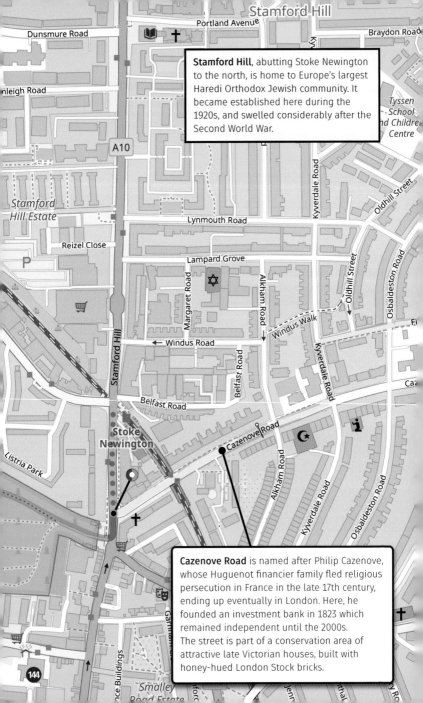

Stamford Hill, abutting Stoke Newington to the north, is home to Europe's largest Haredi Orthodox Jewish community. It became established here during the 1920s, and swelled considerably after the Second World War.

Cazenove Road is named after Philip Cazenove, whose Huguenot financier family fled religious persecution in France in the late 17th century, ending up eventually in London. Here, he founded an investment bank in 1823 which remained independent until the 2000s.
The street is part of a conservation area of attractive late Victorian houses, built with honey-hued London Stock bricks.

Springfield House, otherwise known as the 'White House', is the only one of the three houses to survive, and now serves as the park's café. There are fine views out over the Lea Valley as you pass through the park, which trails down the hillside to the river.

Springfield Park opened in 1905 when the gardens of three private houses were merged. The population of the borough of Hackney increased by 400% in the last 50 years of the 19th century and it took a determined campaign by the owners of the houses and the public to prevent the land being sold for housing development. Roman sarcophagi were found in the park in the 19th century and, more recently, the remains of a Saxon logboat, carved from a single trunk, was discovered close by. It may have been used as a ferry across the Lea.

East London local **Worthington G Smith** was an illustrator, plant pathologist, mushroom expert and amateur archaeologist. It is largely thanks to his pottering around the house and road building sites of Victorian Stoke Newington that we know that Palaeolithic communities were present in the area; he discovered more than 200 complete flint axes.

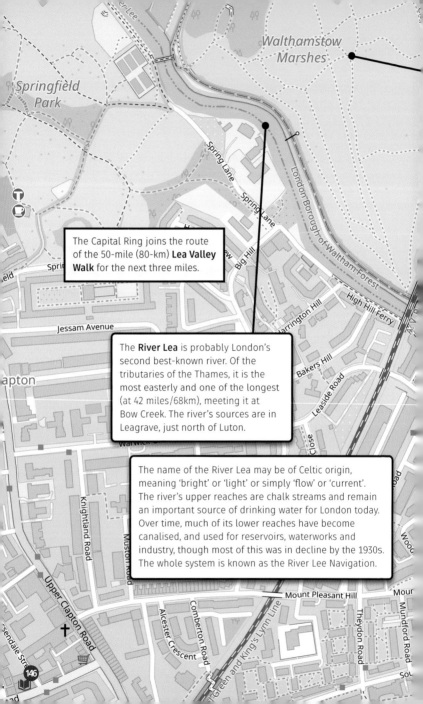

The Capital Ring joins the route of the 50-mile (80-km) **Lea Valley Walk** for the next three miles.

The **River Lea** is probably London's second best-known river. Of the tributaries of the Thames, it is the most easterly and one of the longest (at 42 miles/68km), meeting it at Bow Creek. The river's sources are in Leagrave, just north of Luton.

The name of the River Lea may be of Celtic origin, meaning 'bright' or 'light' or simply 'flow' or 'current'. The river's upper reaches are chalk streams and remain an important source of drinking water for London today. Over time, much of its lower reaches have become canalised, and used for reservoirs, waterworks and industry, though most of this was in decline by the 1930s. The whole system is known as the River Lee Navigation.

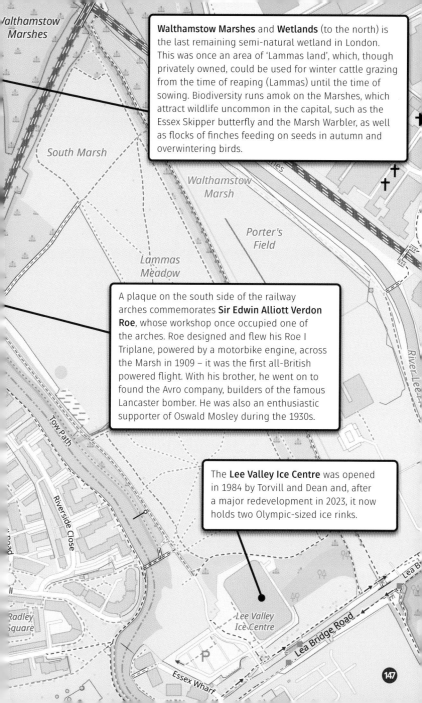

Walthamstow Marshes and **Wetlands** (to the north) is the last remaining semi-natural wetland in London. This was once an area of 'Lammas land', which, though privately owned, could be used for winter cattle grazing from the time of reaping (Lammas) until the time of sowing. Biodiversity runs amok on the Marshes, which attract wildlife uncommon in the capital, such as the Essex Skipper butterfly and the Marsh Warbler, as well as flocks of finches feeding on seeds in autumn and overwintering birds.

A plaque on the south side of the railway arches commemorates **Sir Edwin Alliott Verdon Roe**, whose workshop once occupied one of the arches. Roe designed and flew his Roe I Triplane, powered by a motorbike engine, across the Marsh in 1909 – it was the first all-British powered flight. With his brother, he went on to found the Avro company, builders of the famous Lancaster bomber. He was also an enthusiastic supporter of Oswald Mosley during the 1930s.

The **Lee Valley Ice Centre** was opened in 1984 by Torvill and Dean and, after a major redevelopment in 2023, it now holds two Olympic-sized ice rinks.

Walthamstow Marshes

South Marsh

Walthamstow Marsh

Porter's Field

Lammas Meadow

Tow Path

Riverside Close

Radley Square

Lee Valley Ice Centre

Lea Bridge Road

Essex Wharf

River Lee

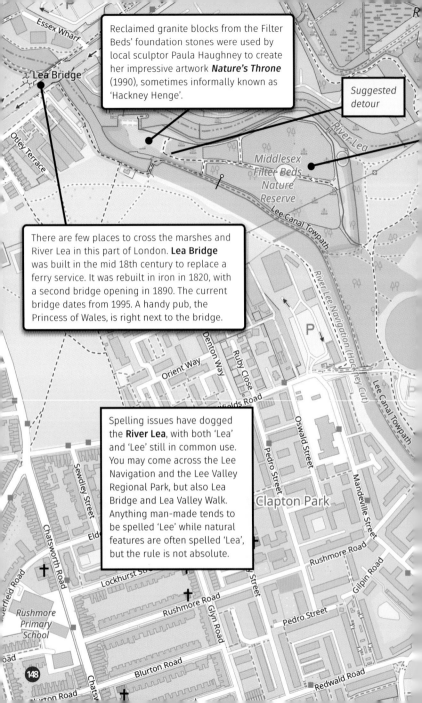

Reclaimed granite blocks from the Filter Beds' foundation stones were used by local sculptor Paula Haughney to create her impressive artwork **Nature's Throne** (1990), sometimes informally known as 'Hackney Henge'.

Suggested detour

There are few places to cross the marshes and River Lea in this part of London. **Lea Bridge** was built in the mid 18th century to replace a ferry service. It was rebuilt in iron in 1820, with a second bridge opening in 1890. The current bridge dates from 1995. A handy pub, the Princess of Wales, is right next to the bridge.

Spelling issues have dogged the **River Lea**, with both 'Lea' and 'Lee' still in common use. You may come across the Lee Navigation and the Lee Valley Regional Park, but also Lea Bridge and Lea Valley Walk. Anything man-made tends to be spelled 'Lee' while natural features are often spelled 'Lea', but the rule is not absolute.

It's well worth a short detour from the river bank to explore the old **Middlesex Filter Beds** (you can rejoin the path a little further on). The beds were built by the East London Water Works company in the mid 19th century to clean up the water supply and help combat cholera, which was killing thousands in Victorian London. As demand outstripped supply, the beds were abandoned in 1969 and the area dried out, but there are plans to bring water back and restore the wetland environment.

This was the original course of the Lea; the **Hackney Cut** to the west was created around 1769 to straighten the river. The two channels join back together two miles (3km) downstream.

Water Jugglers is a striking steel and glass artwork, created in 2004 by Peter Dunn. The images in glass were made by local schools and community groups.

Hackney Marshes is one of the capital's largest areas of common land. The Romans built a stone causeway across the frequently flooded marsh. It passed through the hands of the Knights Templar, then the Knights Hospitaller, then the Crown and eventually into public ownership by the end of the 19th century. Today, Hackney Marshes is best known for its Sunday league football, with 88 full-size pitches.

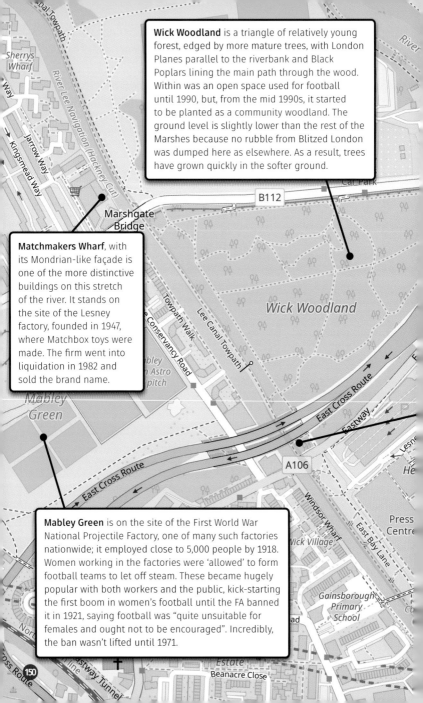

Wick Woodland is a triangle of relatively young forest, edged by more mature trees, with London Planes parallel to the riverbank and Black Poplars lining the main path through the wood. Within was an open space used for football until 1990, but, from the mid 1990s, it started to be planted as a community woodland. The ground level is slightly lower than the rest of the Marshes because no rubble from Blitzed London was dumped here as elsewhere. As a result, trees have grown quickly in the softer ground.

Matchmakers Wharf, with its Mondrian-like façade is one of the more distinctive buildings on this stretch of the river. It stands on the site of the Lesney factory, founded in 1947, where Matchbox toys were made. The firm went into liquidation in 1982 and sold the brand name.

Mabley Green is on the site of the First World War National Projectile Factory, one of many such factories nationwide; it employed close to 5,000 people by 1918. Women working in the factories were 'allowed' to form football teams to let off steam. These became hugely popular with both workers and the public, kick-starting the first boom in women's football until the FA banned it in 1921, saying football was "quite unsuitable for females and ought not to be encouraged". Incredibly, the ban wasn't lifted until 1971.

Wick Woodland

B112

A106

Mabley Green

East Cross Route

Eastway

Towpath Walk

Lee Canal Towpath

Conservancy Road

Windsor Wharf

Wick Village

East Bay Lane

Gainsborough Primary School

Press Centre

Marshgate Bridge

River Lee Navigation (Hackney Cut)

Sherrys Wharf

Jarrow Way

Kingsmead Way

Beanacre Close

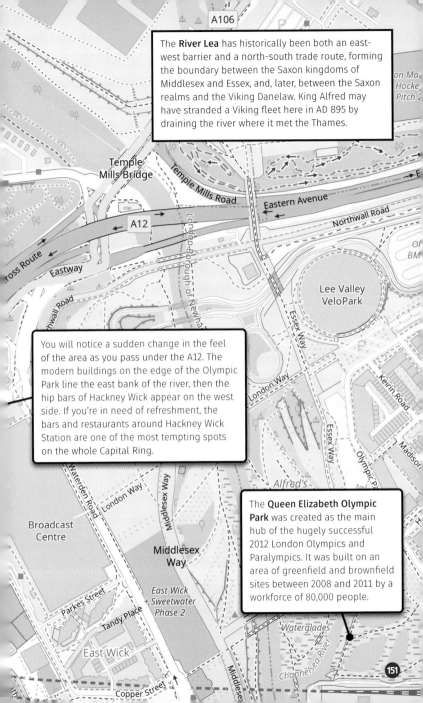

The **River Lea** has historically been both an east-west barrier and a north-south trade route, forming the boundary between the Saxon kingdoms of Middlesex and Essex, and, later, between the Saxon realms and the Viking Danelaw. King Alfred may have stranded a Viking fleet here in AD 895 by draining the river where it met the Thames.

You will notice a sudden change in the feel of the area as you pass under the A12. The modern buildings on the edge of the Olympic Park line the east bank of the river, then the hip bars of Hackney Wick appear on the west side. If you're in need of refreshment, the bars and restaurants around Hackney Wick Station are one of the most tempting spots on the whole Capital Ring.

The **Queen Elizabeth Olympic Park** was created as the main hub of the hugely successful 2012 London Olympics and Paralympics. It was built on an area of greenfield and brownfield sites between 2008 and 2011 by a workforce of 80,000 people.

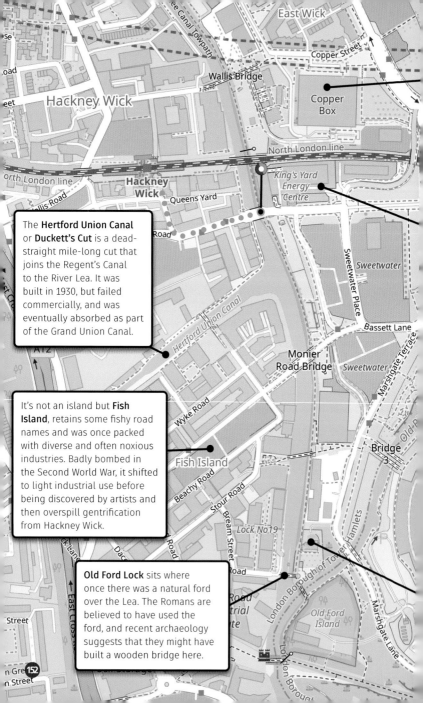

East Wick

Copper Street

Wallis Bridge

Hackney Wick

Copper Box

North London line

orth London line

Hackney Wick

Queens Yard

King's Yard Energy Centre

Sweetwater

Road

The **Hertford Union Canal** or **Duckett's Cut** is a dead-straight mile-long cut that joins the Regent's Canal to the River Lea. It was built in 1930, but failed commercially, and was eventually absorbed as part of the Grand Union Canal.

Sweetwater Place

Bassett Lane

A12

Hertford Union Canal

Monier Road Bridge

Sweetwater

Marshgate Terrace

Wyke Road

Old P

Bridge 3

It's not an island but **Fish Island**, retains some fishy road names and was once packed with diverse and often noxious industries. Badly bombed in the Second World War, it shifted to light industrial use before being discovered by artists and then overspill gentrification from Hackney Wick.

Fish Island

Beachy Road

Stour Road

Bream Street

Lock No19

London Borough of Tower Hamlets

Old Ford Island

East

Road

trial te

Old Ford Lock sits where once there was a natural ford over the Lea. The Romans are believed to have used the ford, and recent archaeology suggests that they might have built a wooden bridge here.

Marshgate Lane

Street

n Gre 152
n Street

London Borough

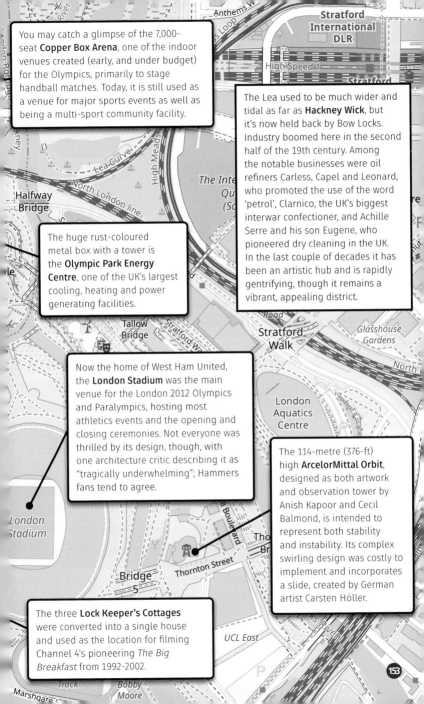

You may catch a glimpse of the 7,000-seat **Copper Box Arena**, one of the indoor venues created (early, and under budget) for the Olympics, primarily to stage handball matches. Today, it is still used as a venue for major sports events as well as being a multi-sport community facility.

The Lea used to be much wider and tidal as far as **Hackney Wick**, but it's now held back by Bow Locks. Industry boomed here in the second half of the 19th century. Among the notable businesses were oil refiners Carless, Capel and Leonard, who promoted the use of the word 'petrol', Clarnico, the UK's biggest interwar confectioner, and Achille Serre and his son Eugene, who pioneered dry cleaning in the UK. In the last couple of decades it has been an artistic hub and is rapidly gentrifying, though it remains a vibrant, appealing district.

The huge rust-coloured metal box with a tower is the **Olympic Park Energy Centre**, one of the UK's largest cooling, heating and power generating facilities.

Now the home of West Ham United, the **London Stadium** was the main venue for the London 2012 Olympics and Paralympics, hosting most athletics events and the opening and closing ceremonies. Not everyone was thrilled by its design, though, with one architecture critic describing it as "tragically underwhelming"; Hammers fans tend to agree.

The 114-metre (376-ft) high **ArcelorMittal Orbit**, designed as both artwork and observation tower by Anish Kapoor and Cecil Balmond, is intended to represent both stability and instability. Its complex swirling design was costly to implement and incorporates a slide, created by German artist Carsten Höller.

The three **Lock Keeper's Cottages** were converted into a single house and used as the location for filming Channel 4's pioneering *The Big Breakfast* from 1992-2002.

153

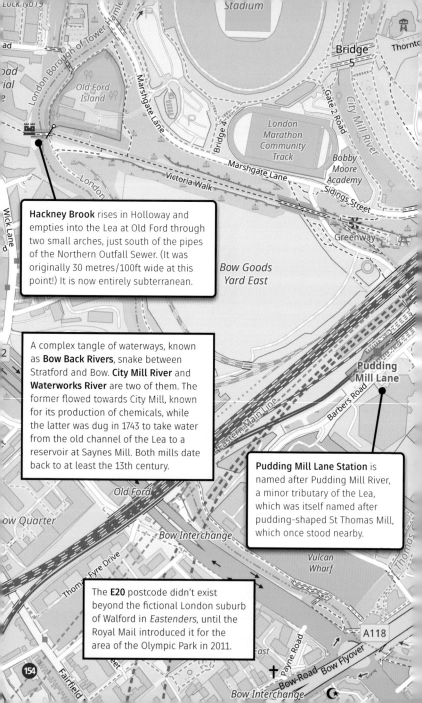

Hackney Brook rises in Holloway and empties into the Lea at Old Ford through two small arches, just south of the pipes of the Northern Outfall Sewer. (It was originally 30 metres/100ft wide at this point!) It is now entirely subterranean.

A complex tangle of waterways, known as **Bow Back Rivers**, snake between Stratford and Bow. **City Mill River** and **Waterworks River** are two of them. The former flowed towards City Mill, known for its production of chemicals, while the latter was dug in 1743 to take water from the old channel of the Lea to a reservoir at Saynes Mill. Both mills date back to at least the 13th century.

Pudding Mill Lane Station is named after Pudding Mill River, a minor tributary of the Lea, which was itself named after pudding-shaped St Thomas Mill, which once stood nearby.

The **E20** postcode didn't exist beyond the fictional London suburb of Walford in *Eastenders*, until the Royal Mail introduced it for the area of the Olympic Park in 2011.

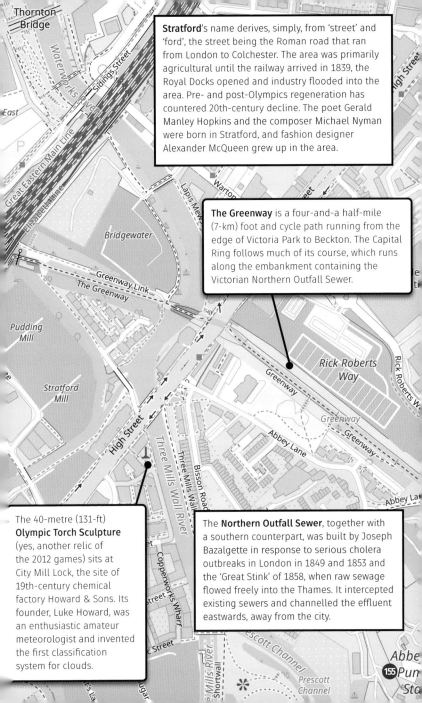

Stratford's name derives, simply, from 'street' and 'ford', the street being the Roman road that ran from London to Colchester. The area was primarily agricultural until the railway arrived in 1839, the Royal Docks opened and industry flooded into the area. Pre- and post-Olympics regeneration has countered 20th-century decline. The poet Gerald Manley Hopkins and the composer Michael Nyman were born in Stratford, and fashion designer Alexander McQueen grew up in the area.

The Greenway is a four-and-a half-mile (7-km) foot and cycle path running from the edge of Victoria Park to Beckton. The Capital Ring follows much of its course, which runs along the embankment containing the Victorian Northern Outfall Sewer.

The 40-metre (131-ft) **Olympic Torch Sculpture** (yes, another relic of the 2012 games) sits at City Mill Lock, the site of 19th-century chemical factory Howard & Sons. Its founder, Luke Howard, was an enthusiastic amateur meteorologist and invented the first classification system for clouds.

The **Northern Outfall Sewer**, together with a southern counterpart, was built by Joseph Bazalgette in response to serious cholera outbreaks in London in 1849 and 1853 and the 'Great Stink' of 1858, when raw sewage flowed freely into the Thames. It intercepted existing sewers and channelled the effluent eastwards, away from the city.

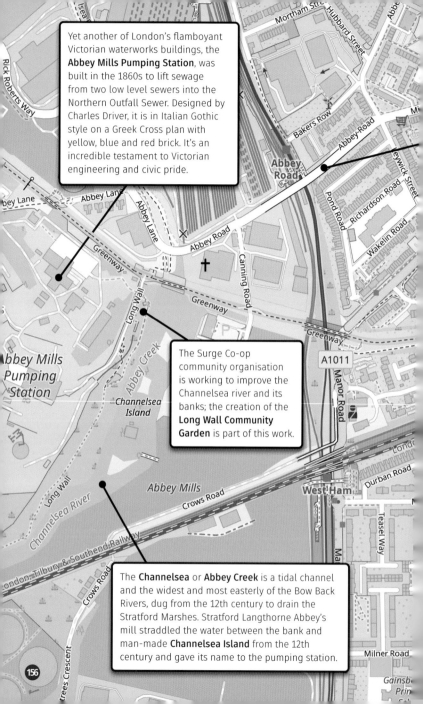

Yet another of London's flamboyant Victorian waterworks buildings, the **Abbey Mills Pumping Station**, was built in the 1860s to lift sewage from two low level sewers into the Northern Outfall Sewer. Designed by Charles Driver, it is in Italian Gothic style on a Greek Cross plan with yellow, blue and red brick. It's an incredible testament to Victorian engineering and civic pride.

The Surge Co-op community organisation is working to improve the Channelsea river and its banks; the creation of the **Long Wall Community Garden** is part of this work.

The **Channelsea** or **Abbey Creek** is a tidal channel and the widest and most easterly of the Bow Back Rivers, dug from the 12th century to drain the Stratford Marshes. Stratford Langthorne Abbey's mill straddled the water between the bank and man-made **Channelsea Island** from the 12th century and gave its name to the pumping station.

Abbey Road in St John's Wood's may be the better-known street these days, but its West Ham namesake remembers what was once one of the largest abbeys in England. **Stratford Langthorne Abbey** was a Cistercian monastery, founded in 1135. No visible trace of it remains, though excavations have discovered extensive burials. A community garden, **Abbey Gardens**, has been created on the site on Bakers Row.

The Old English word 'Hamme' means 'dry land between rivers and marshes'. The Manor of Ham, between the Lea, Thames and Roding, is mentioned in an Anglo-Saxon charter of 958. It had been split into West and East Ham by the late 12th century. From the mid 19th century, **West Ham** rapidly urbanised and industrialised; most of the heavy industry had gone by the 1970s.

East London Cemetery was founded in 1871 to cope with the burgeoning local population. It include a memorial to the 550 victims of the *SS Princess Alice* disaster on the Thames, the country's worst ever inland waterway shipping accident, as well as the graves of Jack the Ripper victim Elizabeth Stride, actress Beryl Cooke, German First World War spy Carl Hans Lody and Blair Peach, the anti-racist activist killed during a protest in 1979.

London's population density has tripled since Bazalgette's time, and his sewer system can no longer cope. To solve the problem, the £4+billion **Thames Tideway Tunnel** 'Super Sewer' has been constructed and is due to open in 2025. It runs for 16 miles (25km) from Acton to Abbey Mills, then on to Beckton where the sewage will be treated before being released into the Thames.

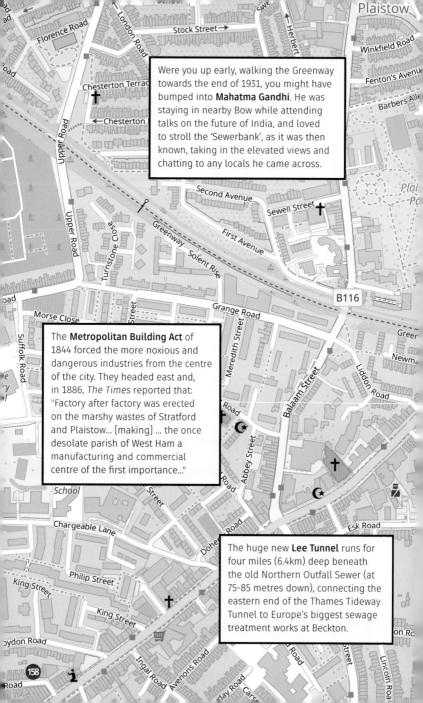

Were you up early, walking the Greenway towards the end of 1931, you might have bumped into **Mahatma Gandhi**. He was staying in nearby Bow while attending talks on the future of India, and loved to stroll the 'Sewerbank', as it was then known, taking in the elevated views and chatting to any locals he came across.

The **Metropolitan Building Act** of 1844 forced the more noxious and dangerous industries from the centre of the city. They headed east and, in 1886, *The Times* reported that: "Factory after factory was erected on the marshy wastes of Stratford and Plaistow... [making] ... the once desolate parish of West Ham a manufacturing and commercial centre of the first importance..."

The huge new **Lee Tunnel** runs for four miles (6.4km) deep beneath the old Northern Outfall Sewer (at 75-85 metres down), connecting the eastern end of the Thames Tideway Tunnel to Europe's biggest sewage treatment works at Beckton.

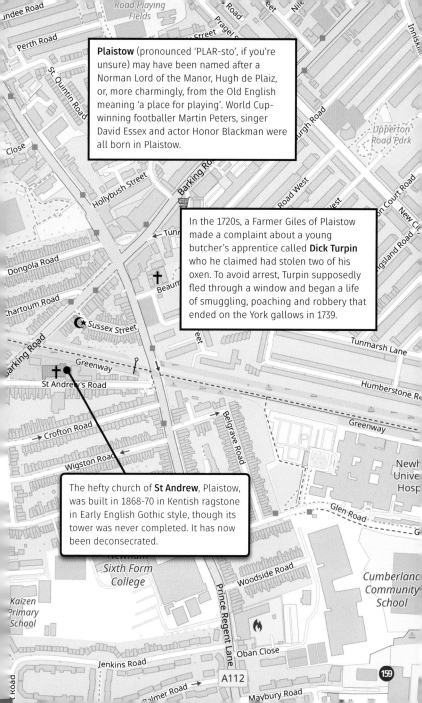

Plaistow (pronounced 'PLAR-sto', if you're unsure) may have been named after a Norman Lord of the Manor, Hugh de Plaiz, or, more charmingly, from the Old English meaning 'a place for playing'. World Cup-winning footballer Martin Peters, singer David Essex and actor Honor Blackman were all born in Plaistow.

In the 1720s, a Farmer Giles of Plaistow made a complaint about a young butcher's apprentice called **Dick Turpin** who he claimed had stolen two of his oxen. To avoid arrest, Turpin supposedly fled through a window and began a life of smuggling, poaching and robbery that ended on the York gallows in 1739.

The hefty church of **St Andrew**, Plaistow, was built in 1868-70 in Kentish ragstone in Early English Gothic style, though its tower was never completed. It has now been deconsecrated.

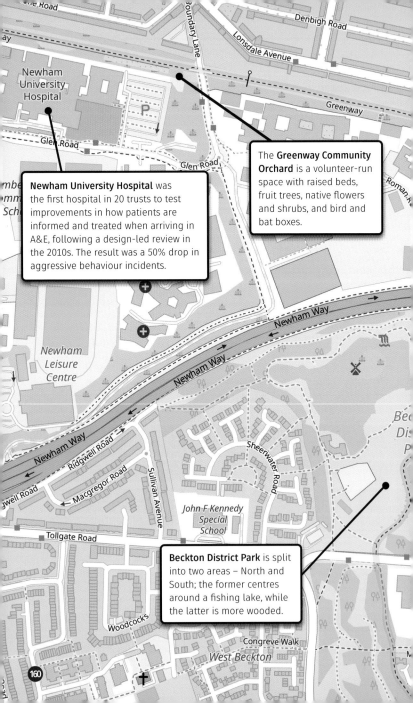

Newham University Hospital was the first hospital in 20 trusts to test improvements in how patients are informed and treated when arriving in A&E, following a design-led review in the 2010s. The result was a 50% drop in aggressive behaviour incidents.

The **Greenway Community Orchard** is a volunteer-run space with raised beds, fruit trees, native flowers and shrubs, and bird and bat boxes.

Beckton District Park is split into two areas – North and South; the former centres around a fishing lake, while the latter is more wooded.

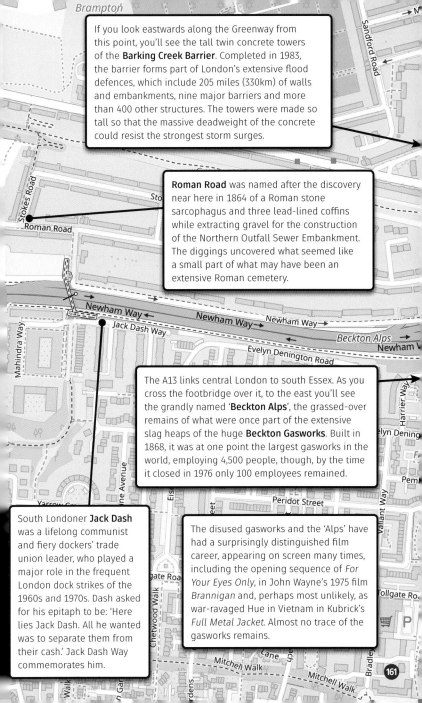

If you look eastwards along the Greenway from this point, you'll see the tall twin concrete towers of the **Barking Creek Barrier**. Completed in 1983, the barrier forms part of London's extensive flood defences, which include 205 miles (330km) of walls and embankments, nine major barriers and more than 400 other structures. The towers were made so tall so that the massive deadweight of the concrete could resist the strongest storm surges.

Roman Road was named after the discovery near here in 1864 of a Roman stone sarcophagus and three lead-lined coffins while extracting gravel for the construction of the Northern Outfall Sewer Embankment. The diggings uncovered what seemed like a small part of what may have been an extensive Roman cemetery.

The A13 links central London to south Essex. As you cross the footbridge over it, to the east you'll see the grandly named '**Beckton Alps**', the grassed-over remains of what were once part of the extensive slag heaps of the huge **Beckton Gasworks**. Built in 1868, it was at one point the largest gasworks in the world, employing 4,500 people, though, by the time it closed in 1976 only 100 employees remained.

South Londoner **Jack Dash** was a lifelong communist and fiery dockers' trade union leader, who played a major role in the frequent London dock strikes of the 1960s and 1970s. Dash asked for his epitaph to be: 'Here lies Jack Dash. All he wanted was to separate them from their cash.' Jack Dash Way commemorates him.

The disused gasworks and the 'Alps' have had a surprisingly distinguished film career, appearing on screen many times, including the opening sequence of *For Your Eyes Only*, in John Wayne's 1975 film *Brannigan* and, perhaps most unlikely, as war-ravaged Hue in Vietnam in Kubrick's *Full Metal Jacket*. Almost no trace of the gasworks remains.

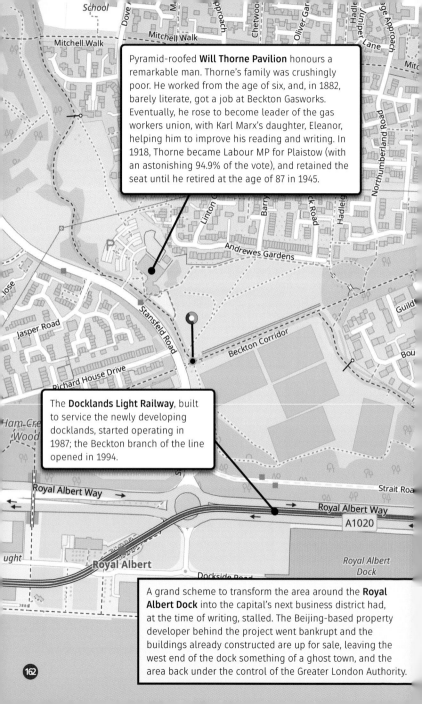

Pyramid-roofed **Will Thorne Pavilion** honours a remarkable man. Thorne's family was crushingly poor. He worked from the age of six, and, in 1882, barely literate, got a job at Beckton Gasworks. Eventually, he rose to become leader of the gas workers union, with Karl Marx's daughter, Eleanor, helping him to improve his reading and writing. In 1918, Thorne became Labour MP for Plaistow (with an astonishing 94.9% of the vote), and retained the seat until he retired at the age of 87 in 1945.

The **Docklands Light Railway**, built to service the newly developing docklands, started operating in 1987; the Beckton branch of the line opened in 1994.

A grand scheme to transform the area around the **Royal Albert Dock** into the capital's next business district had, at the time of writing, stalled. The Beijing-based property developer behind the project went bankrupt and the buildings already constructed are up for sale, leaving the west end of the dock something of a ghost town, and the area back under the control of the Greater London Authority.

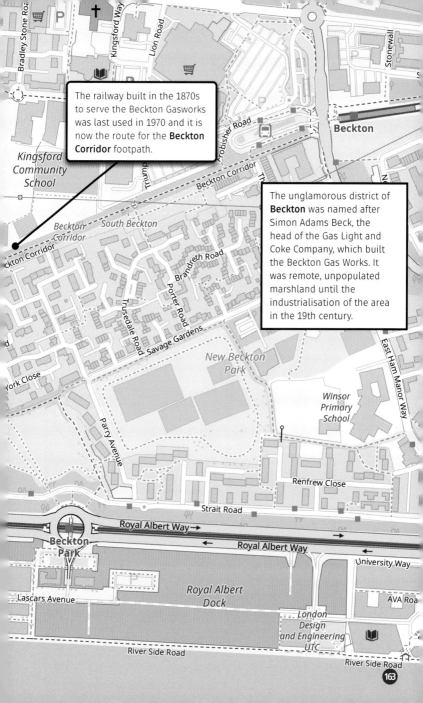

The railway built in the 1870s to serve the Beckton Gasworks was last used in 1970 and it is now the route for the **Beckton Corridor** footpath.

The unglamorous district of **Beckton** was named after Simon Adams Beck, the head of the Gas Light and Coke Company, which built the Beckton Gas Works. It was remote, unpopulated marshland until the industrialisation of the area in the 19th century.

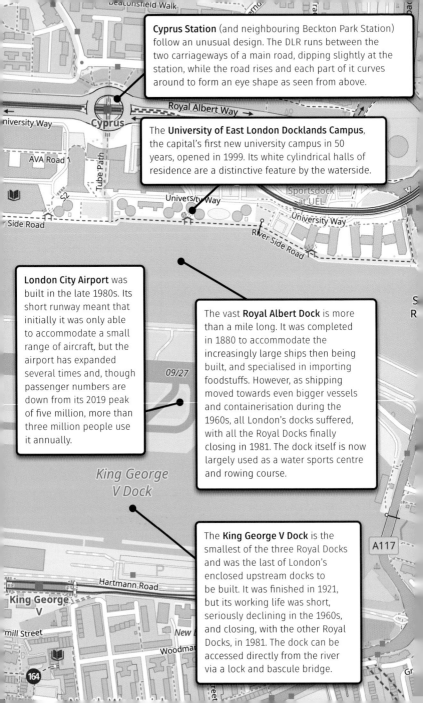

Cyprus Station (and neighbouring Beckton Park Station) follow an unusual design. The DLR runs between the two carriageways of a main road, dipping slightly at the station, while the road rises and each part of it curves around to form an eye shape as seen from above.

The **University of East London Docklands Campus**, the capital's first new university campus in 50 years, opened in 1999. Its white cylindrical halls of residence are a distinctive feature by the waterside.

London City Airport was built in the late 1980s. Its short runway meant that initially it was only able to accommodate a small range of aircraft, but the airport has expanded several times and, though passenger numbers are down from its 2019 peak of five million, more than three million people use it annually.

The vast **Royal Albert Dock** is more than a mile long. It was completed in 1880 to accommodate the increasingly large ships then being built, and specialised in importing foodstuffs. However, as shipping moved towards even bigger vessels and containerisation during the 1960s, all London's docks suffered, with all the Royal Docks finally closing in 1981. The dock itself is now largely used as a water sports centre and rowing course.

The **King George V Dock** is the smallest of the three Royal Docks and was the last of London's enclosed upstream docks to be built. It was finished in 1921, but its working life was short, seriously declining in the 1960s, and closing, with the other Royal Docks, in 1981. The dock can be accessed directly from the river via a lock and bascule bridge.

The **Gallions Hotel** (now a bar/restaurant), once known locally as 'The Captain's Brothel', was built in the 1880s and featured a tunnel that allowed officers and passengers to access their ships waiting in the dock. The young Rudyard Kipling, heading to India, was one of them, and mentioned the hotel in his novel *The Light That Failed*.

The **Royal Docks Pumping Station**, built in 1912, houses four huge pumps to help manage water levels within the docks, drawing water from the Thames.

Suggested detour

Cyprus may seem a curious name for a sub-area of Beckton. It comes from the Cyprus Estate, which opened in 1881 to house workers from the docks and gasworks. The estate was named to commemorate the UK taking control of the island of Cyprus from the Ottoman Empire in 1878. Most of the estate was destroyed in the Blitz but, in the early 1980s, it became the site of the London Docklands Development Corporation's first housing development. Its success prompted further residential development across the docklands.

The route is occasionally closed here when the lock is in operation, and you can divert across Albert Island instead.

Map labels:
Gallions Reach
Atlantis Avenue
Gallions Point
Royal Quay Road
Gallions Road
Gallions
Gallions Point
Hudson
Upper Dock Walk
Lower Dock Walk
Gallions Point Marina
Lockside Way
Albert Island
Albert Island
Capital Ring
Fishguard Way
Gallions
London Borough of Newham

The **Royal Victoria Gardens** were laid out as a Victorian pleasure garden in 1850 by the owner of the nearby Pavilion Hotel and drew in large crowds to attractions that included "a maze, gipsy's tent, rifle gallery, ballroom and refreshment room". Re-opened as a park by the council in 1890, it was, until the 1960s, rather oddly officially part of Kent, despite being surrounded by Essex.

The **Woolwich Foot Tunnel** was designed by Irish engineer Sir Maurice Fitzmaurice, who was also responsible for the Blackwall and Rotherhithe tunnels, and, more surprisingly, the Aswan Dam. Its creation, in 1912, to provide all-weather access for dockworkers from Woolwich, was down in large part to the efforts of former dockworker, Will Crooks, who would later become Labour MP for Woolwich. Walking its eerie 504-metre (1,654-ft) length is a fittingly memorable way to complete the Capital Ring.

The **old pier** was once used by steamers operated by the Eastern Counties Railway to aid their passengers from nearby North Woolwich station (now closed and demolished) who wanted to cross the Thames.

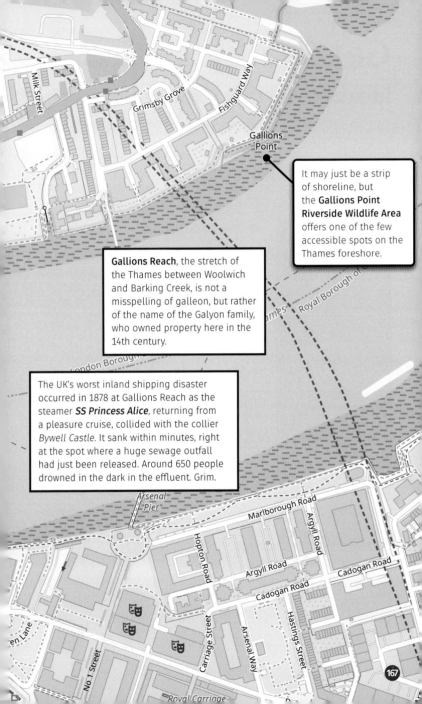

It may just be a strip of shoreline, but the **Gallions Point Riverside Wildlife Area** offers one of the few accessible spots on the Thames foreshore.

Gallions Reach, the stretch of the Thames between Woolwich and Barking Creek, is not a misspelling of galleon, but rather of the name of the Galyon family, who owned property here in the 14th century.

The UK's worst inland shipping disaster occurred in 1878 at Gallions Reach as the steamer **SS Princess Alice**, returning from a pleasure cruise, collided with the collier *Bywell Castle*. It sank within minutes, right at the spot where a huge sewage outfall had just been released. Around 650 people drowned in the dark in the effluent. Grim.

Get Sparky!
Ideas for further exploration

If your curiosity has been sparked and you have been inspired by your walking to delve deeper into some of the topics relevant to the Capital Ring, here are a few resources we found useful.

→ The Capital Ring

Inner London Ramblers – *innerlondonramblers.org.uk*

Part of the national Ramblers organisation, this website offers downloadable guides to the standard 15 stages, though these focus primarily on directions rather than the riches to be discovered along the way. It also has an excellent guide to accessibility on the Capital Ring and updates on issues along the route.

→ History of London

A History of London by Stephen Inwood (Macmillan, 1998)

The compelling complexity of London is superbly drawn in Inwood's immense, vivid survey of the capital's history.

Lights Out for the Territory by Iain Sinclair (Granta, 1997; Penguin, 2003)

Sinclair's seminal, idiosyncratic book traces nine unglamorous routes across the capital in the 1990s, bringing out the strange and fascinating in the everyday and painting a vivid 'psychogeography' of London.

London: The Biography by Peter Ackroyd (Chatto & Windus, 2000)

Still a classic, Ackroyd's 'biography' eschews a chronological approach for a thematic one that builds into an elaborate and incomparably rich picture of London through time.

East London History – *eastlondonhistory.co.uk*

This blogsite by Malcolm Oakley is a great source of historical info on the East End, from West Ham Football Club to Beckton Gas Works.

The Enthusiastic Gardener – *enthusiasticgardener.com*

Candy Blackham's lovely, quirky website focuses on parks and gardens, with particularly interesting pages on parks within the boroughs of Greenwich and Lewisham.

Hidden London – *hidden-london.com*

The Hidden London website, created by Russ Willey, is a fantastic resource for those who like to poke around in the city's less well-known corners, featuring more than 750 articles on different metropolitan localities.

The History of London – *thehistoryoflondon.co.uk*

A wide-ranging and authoritative website by Peter Stone, which delves into many intriguing aspects of the history of London's places and people, and is particularly strong on the Port of London.

London's Lost Rivers – *londonslostrivers.com*

Paul Talling's fascinating website (and associated book) tells the often forgotten stories of the capital's watercourses, many of which are little known.

➔ London people

Below is a highly selective collection of references to individuals who feature prominently along the Capital Ring route.

Joseph Bazalgette

The Great Stink of London: Sir Joseph Bazalgette and the Cleansing of the Victorian Metropolis by Stephen Halliday (Sutton Publishing, 1999)

The detailed story of how Bazalgette transformed the sewer system and, consequently, health of London.

Archibald Corbett

thecorbettsociety.org.uk

A nice introduction to Archibald Corbett, his background, and his legacy in philanthropy and housing development in London.

Daniel Defoe

tinyurl.com/danieldefoeinlondon

An interesting overview of Defoe's varied, colourful and often tumultuous life in the city.

Charles Holden

London Tube Stations 1924-1961 by Phillip Butler and Joshua Abbott (FUEL, 2023)

Holden's work in the capital is photographed and documented alongside many other architects in this attractive photobook.

tinyurl.com/charlesholdeninlondon

The London Transport Museum's easy-to-read but fascinating illustrated guide to one of the key architects of London Underground stations.

Joseph Paxton

A Thing in Disguise: The Visionary Life of Joseph Paxton by Kate Colquhoun (Harper Perennial, 2009)

An excellent biography of the designer of the Crystal Palace and his remarkable career.

William Perkins Warner

tinyurl.com/OldWelshHarp

An entertaining article by Philip Grant on the remarkable landlord of the Old Welsh Harp who made his tavern by Brent Reservoir a go-to Victorian leisure destination.

➡ Churches

English Churches Explained by Trevor Yorke (Countryside Books, 2010)

This compact, well-illustrated guide covers English church architecture and interiors from the Saxon to Victorian eras.

Historic English Churches: A Guide to their Construction, Design and Features by Geoffrey R Sharpe (Bloomsbury Academic, 2020)

A hugely detailed and authoritative analysis with separate sections on construction, architecture and church interiors.

tinyurl.com/britishchurches

A nicely detailed guide that brings history and description together to create a good illustrated journey through British church development.

visitchurches.org.uk

The Churches Conservation Trust provides this easy-to-use database of churches across the country, searchable by name or location.

→ Flora and fauna

Collins Complete Guide to British Insects
by Michael Chinery (Collins, 2009)

Close to 400 pages covering over 1,500 species and where to find them.

butterfly-conservation.org

Bags of fascinating information to help you identify the 57 native butterfly species (and two regular migrants) plus many of our 2,500+ moth species.

wildflowerfinder.org.uk

A comprehensive database of wildflowers in the UK and Ireland, searchable by colour, month, habitat, number of petals and other parameters.

wildlifetrusts.org/wildlife-explorer

An excellent source of information on the UK's native species, organised into 14 sections including wildflowers, fungi, trees and shrubs, birds, invertebrates and mammals.

There is a wealth of apps available to help you identify birds, insects, plants and trees. For birds, we like Merlin and Picture Bird. Good plant and tree ID apps include Pl@ntNet, PictureThis and LeafSnap.

➜ Local societies & sites

Beckenham Place Park

Friend of Beckenham Place Park –
beckenhamplaceparkfriends.org.uk

Brentford

Brent River Park – *brentriverpark.org*

Brentford & Chiswick Local History Society –
brentfordandchiswicklhs.org.uk

Syon House – *syonpark.co.uk*

Charlton

Charlton House & Gardens – *tinyurl.com/charltonhouseandgardens*

The Charlton Society – *charltonsociety.org*

Friends of Maryon Park and Maryon Wilson Park –
friendsofmaryonparks.org

Crystal Palace

The Crystal Palace Foundation –
crystalpalacefoundation.org.uk

Crystal Palace Park Trust – *crystalpalaceparktrust.org*

Friends of Crystal Palace Dinosaurs – *cpdinosaurs.org*

Eltham

Eltham Palace & Gardens – *tinyurl.com/eltham-palace-and-gardens*

The Eltham Society – *theelthamsociety.org.uk*

Finsbury Park

Friends of Finsbury Park –
thefriendsoffinsburypark.org.uk

Fryent Country Park

Barn Hill Conservation Group –
barnhillconservationgroup.org

Hampstead Garden Suburb

Hampstead Garden Suburb Heritage –
hgsheritage.org.uk

Highgate

The Highgate Society – *highgatesociety.com*

Isleworth

The Isleworth Society – *isleworthsociety.org*

Norwood

Friends of Biggin Wood – *friendsofbigginwood.org*

The Norwood Society – *norwoodsociety.co.uk*

Norwood Street Histories – *norwoodstreethistories.org.uk*

Oxleas Woodlands

Friends of Oxleas Woodlands – *oxleaswoodlands.uk*

Parkland Walk

Friends of the Parkland Walk – *parkland-walk.org.uk*

Richmond

Friends of Richmond Park – *frp.org.uk*

The Richmond Society – *richmondsociety.org.uk*

Royal Docks

London's Royal Docks – *londonsroyaldocks.com*

Stoke Newington

Abney Park Trust – *abneypark.org*

Clissold Park User Group – *clissoldpark.com*

Stratford

Queen Elizabeth Olympic Park – *queenelizabetholympicpark.co.uk*

Streatham

Friends of Streatham Common – *streathamcommon.org*

The Streatham Society – *streathamsociety.org.uk*

Tooting

Tooting History Group – *tootinghistory.org.uk*

Friends of Tooting Common – *friendsoftootingcommon.uk*

Walthamstow Marshes

Walthamstow Marshes – *visitleevalley.org.uk/walthamstow-marshes*

Wandsworth

Friends of Wandsworth Common – *wandsworthcommon.org*

The Wandsworth Society – *wandsworthsociety.org*

Welsh Harp/Brent Reservoir

Friends of the Welsh Harp – *welshharpfriends.co.uk*

Wembley

History of Wembley (area) – *tinyurl.com/wembleyhistory*

History of Wembley Stadium – *tinyurl.com/wembleystadiumhistory*

Wimbledon

Friends of Wimbledon Park – *friendsofwimbledonpark.org*

Wimbledon & Putney Commons – *wpcc.org.uk*

Woodberry Wetlands

London Wildlife Trust – *tinyurl.com/woodberry-wetlands*

Woolwich

Friends of Woolwich Common – *friendsofwoolwichcommon.org.uk*

Royal Arsenal History – *royal-arsenal-history.com*

➜ Railways

ltmuseum.co.uk

The London Transport Museum website is packed with information about the development of the city's transport network, including the development of the Underground network, the promotion of 'Metro-land', the suburban expansion of the city along the route of the Metropolitan Railway, and Charles Holden, designer of many iconic Tube stations

tinyurl.com/railwaynetwork

Although academic in origin, this is an easily read and understood illustrated description of the growth of the railway network in its heyday in Britain between 1825 and 1911.

➜ Sites, monuments and buildings

Hidden Histories: A Spotter's Guide to the British Landscape by Mary-Ann Ochota (Frances Lincoln, 2018 reprint)

A well-illustrated and easy-to-dip-in-and-out-of guide on much of what you see in the landscape, from earthworks, standing stones and barrows to pub names, types of trees and basic village development.

Pevsner Architectural Guides series by Nikolaus Pevsner (Yale University Press)

The original series of the classic County-based architectural guides by art historian Pevnser and collaborators were published between the 1950s and 1970s. Most have been updated and expanded since and are still in print.

britishlistedbuildings.co.uk

An online database of buildings and sites listed for their special historic or architectural interest.

finds.org.uk

The British Museum's Portable Antiquities Scheme website details the thousands of finds made by members of the public in England and Wales every year.

heritagegateway.org.uk

Historic England's Heritage Gateway provides access to more than 60 databases detailing historic sites and buildings in England.

➡ Woodlands

Oak and Ash and Thorn by Peter Fiennes
(Oneworld Publications, 2018)

An intriguing and entertaining blend of natural
history, folklore, botany and opinion, this is also
a story of the rise and fall of woodlands in Britain
over time.

Woodlands by Oliver Rackham (Collins, 2015)

Part of the New Naturalist series of natural history
books, this is a detailed guide to woodlands through
the ages including their care and management, basic
botany and how to study them.

woodlandtrust.org.uk

The perfect starting-point for everything woodland in
the UK; the range and breadth of information within
the Trust's website is impressive.

Flora & fauna

Spotting and identifying wildlife and plants is one of the great joys of walking. To help you differentiate your Timothy from your Velvet Bent from your Yorkshire Fog, here are pictures of all the flora and fauna we mention in the guide.

➔ Flowers & grasses

Bluebell
Hyacinthoides non-scripta

Bog Bean
Menyanthes trifoliata

Broom
Cytisus scoparius

Common Butterwort
Pinguicula vulgaris

Crested Dog's-tail
Cynosurus cristatus

False Oat-grass
Arrhenatherum elatius

Mouse-ear Hawkweed
Pilosella officinarum

Timothy
Phleum pratense

Tormentil
Potentilla erecta

Velvet Bent
Agrostis canina

White Water-lily
Nymphaea alba

Wood Anemone
Anemone nemorosa

Wood Spurge
Euphorbia amygdaloides

Yellow Pimpernel
Lysimachia nemorum

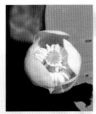

Yellow Water-lily
Nuphar lutea

Yorkshire Fog
Holcus lanatus

Alder
Alnus glutinosa

Ash
Fraxinus excelsior

Beech
Fagus sylvatica

Black Mulberry
Morus nigra

Black Poplar
Populus nigra

Blackthorn
Prunus spinosa

Crack Willow
Salix fragilis

Field Maple
Acer campestre

Giant Sequoia
Sequoiadendron giganteum

Grey Willow
Salix cinerea

Hawthorn
Crataegus monogyna

Highclere Holly
Ilex x altaclerensis

Holly
Ilex aquifolium

Hornbeam
Carpinus betulus

Horse Chestnut
Aesculus hippocastanum

London Plane
Platanus x hispanica

Penduculate (English) Oak
Quercus robur

Silver Birch
Betula pendula

Sweet Chestnut
Castanea sativa

Wild Plum
Prunus domestica

Wild Service Tree
Sorbus torminalis

Yew
Taxus baccata

Bats

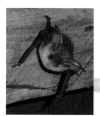

Brown Long-eared
Plecotus auritus

Daubenton's
Myotis daubentonii

Leisler's
Nyctalus leisleri

Nathusius' Pipistrelle
Pipistrellus nathusii

Pipistrelle
Pipistrellus pipistrellus

Birds

Barn Swallow
Hirundo rustica

Bittern
Botaurus stellaris

Blackcap
Sylvia atricapilla

Chiffchaff
Phylloscopus collybita

Common Swift
Apus apus

Common Tern
Sterna hirundo

Coot
Fulica atra

Egyptian Goose
Alopochen aegyptiaca

Eurasian Wigeon
Mareca Penelope

Goldcrest
Regulus regulus

Great Crested Grebe
Podiceps cristatus

Great Spotted Woodpecker
Dendrocopos major

Grey Heron
Ardea cinerea

Hobby
Falco Subbuteo

Kingfisher
Alcedo atthis

Lesser Spotted Woodpecker
Dendrocopos minor

Little Egret
Egretta garzetta

Mallard
Anas platyrhynchos

Mandarin Duck
Aix galericulata

Marsh Tit
Poecile palustris

Moorhen
Gallinula chloropus

Redpoll
Carduelis flammea

Reed Bunting
Emberiza schoeniclus

Reed Warbler
Acrocephalus scirpaceus

Rose-ringed Parakeet
Psittacula krameri

Tufted Duck
Aythya fuligula

➔ Insects & molluscs

Essex Skipper
Thymelicus lineola

German Hairy Snail
Pseudotrichia rubiginosa

Hawthorn Jewel Beetle
Agrilus sinuatus

Roesel's Bush-cricket
Metrioptera roeselii

Stag Beetle
Lucanus cervus

Yellow Meadow Ant
Lasius flavus

→ Other animals

Brown Trout
Salmo trutta

Eurasian Beaver
Castor fiber

European Eel
Anguilla Anguilla

Fallow Deer
Dama dama

Muntjac Deer
Muntiacus reevesi

Red Deer
Cervus elaphus

Slow-worm
Anguis fragilis

Photo credits

Photos by Jon Cox, with the exception of those listed below, which were sourced from Wikimedia Commons (commons.wikimedia.org).

Inside back throwout:
Peter O'Connor aka anemoneprojectors, CC BY-SA-2.0

page 178
MichaelMaggs, CC BY-SA 3.0; Krzysztof Ziarnek, Kenraiz, CC BY-SA 4.0; Willow, CC BY-SA 3.0; Björn S..., CC BY-SA 2.0; Robert Flogaus-Faust, CC BY 4.0; Krzysztof Ziarnek, Kenraiz, CC BY-SA 4.0; Christopher Stephens, CC BY-SA 4.0; Michel Langeveld, CC BY-SA 4.0

page 179
Robert Flogaus-Faust, CC BY 4.0; James Lindsey at Ecology of Commanster, CC BY-SA 2.5; Fernando Losada Rodríguez, CC BY-SA 4.0; Uoaei1, CC BY-SA 4.0; Andy Morffew from Itchen Abbas, Hampshire, UK, CC BY 2.0; Phil Sellens from East Sussex, CC BY 2.0; Uoaei1, CC BY-SA 4.0; Franz Xaver, CC BY-SA 3.0

page 180
Michel Langeveld, CC BY-SA 4.0; Agnieszka Kwiecień, Nova, CC BY-SA 4.0; Lidine Mia, CC BY-SA 4.0; DS28, CC BY-SA 4.0; Krzysztof Ziarnek, Kenraiz, CC BY-SA 4.0; Arnstein Rønning, CC BY-SA 3.0; Krzysztof Ziarnek, Kenraiz, CC BY-SA 4.0; Josep Gesti, CC BY-SA 4.0; Jdforrester, CC BY-SA 3.0; Roland.aprent, CC BY-SA 4.0; AudreyMuratet, CC BY-SA 4.0

page 181
A. Barra, CC BY 3.0; Peter Andersen, CC BY 4.0; Agnieszka Kwiecień, Nova, CC BY-SA 4.0; Agnieszka Kwiecień, Nova, CC BY-SA 4.0; Luis Fernández García, CC BY-SA 4.0; Robert Flogaus-Faust, CC BY 4.0; Andrew Butko, CC BY-SA 3.0; Auckland Museum, CC BY 4.0; Anastasiia Merkulova, CC BY 4.0; Krzysztof Ziarnek, Kenraiz, CC BY-SA 4.0; MAKY.OREL, CC0 1.0

page 182
Tommy Andriollo, CC BY 4.0; Gilles San Martin from Namur, Belgium, CC BY-SA 2.0; Manuel Sánchez de Frutos, GPL; Mnolf, CC BY-SA 3.0; Gilles San Martin from Namur, Belgium, CC BY-SA 2.0; Andrew Bazdyrev, CC BY 4.0; caroline legg, CC BY 2.0; Ron Knight from Seaford, East Sussex, United Kingdom, CC BY 2.0; Andreas Trepte, CC BY-SA 2.5; Marton Berntsen, CC BY-SA 3.0; Zeynel Cebeci, CC BY-SA 4.0

page 183
Alexis Lours, CC BY 4.0; Charles J. Sharp, CC BY-SA 4.0; Tisha Mukherjee, CC BY-SA 4.0; Cj Hughson from Shetland, CC BY 2.0; Ken Billington, CC BY-SA 3.0; Bengt Nyman from Vaxholm, Sweden, CC BY 2.0; JJ Harrison, CC BY-SA 3.0; Imran Shah from Islamabad, Pakistan, CC BY-SA 2.0; Andreas Trepte, CC BY-SA 2.5; Ron Knight from Seaford, East Sussex, United Kingdom, CC BY 2.0; El Golli Mohamed, CC BY-SA 4.0

page 184
Richard Bartz, CC BY-SA 2.5; Francis C. Franklin, CC-BY-SA-3.0; Ken Billington, CC BY-SA 3.0; Monkey Boy from Johannesburg, South Africa, CC BY-SA 2.0; Cephas, CC BY-SA 3.0; MPF, CC BY-SA 4.0; Ron Knight, CC BY 2.0; Charles J. Sharp, CC BY-SA 4.0; Alexis Lours, CC BY 4.0; Michel Langeveld, CC BY-SA 4.0; Roman Hural, CC BY-SA 4.0; James Lindsey at Ecology of Commanster, CC BY-SA 2.5

page 185
Richard Bartz, Munich aka Makro Freak, CC BY-SA 2.5; Syrio, CC BY-SA 4.0; Andy Murray, CC BY-SA 2.0; Eric Engbretson for U.S. Fish and Wildlife Service, Public domain; Colorado State University Libraries, CC BY-SA 4.0; GerardM, CC BY-SA 3.0; Johann-Nikolaus Andreae, CC BY-SA 2.0 sarefo, CC BY-SA 3.0; Lviatour, CC BY-SA 3.0; Holger Krisp, CC BY 3.0

Index

Main entries are in **bold**;
photographs are in *italics*